Tattered Scrolls and Postulates:
Volume I

Poems, Viscera, Encyclopedia, Esoterica

Joseph V. Milford

Backlash Press

A pioneering publishing house dedicated to creating intelligent, vivid books. Established to inform, educate, entertain and provoke.

A Backlash Press Book
First published 2017

www.backlashpress.com

SCB Distributors
15608 South New Century Drive
Gardena, CA 90248, USA

Cover designer: The Scrutineer, Rachael Adams.
Photographer: Tiffany Bayona

Printed and bound by Ingram.

ISBN: 978-0-9955999-1-8

For Papa Joe, Red, Marvene, and Louise

By the same author

Cracked Altimeter

Reviews

I have been hammered like a precious metal used for battle begins one section of Joe Milford's ultra rich book of 1000 lines. John Ashbery suggested that one way is to put it all in; in Tattered Scrolls and Postulates, what we find is one version of what happens when a mind is so filled up with the love of what language makes that it spills non-stop like a blue streak of poetry fleeing before mortality bites its heels; and yes, that's a little mixed up and that's how it has to be. Take this book a page at a time, take it slowly, you know, the way the speed of light can only be understood when it's just beyond reach.

Dara Weir, author of You Good Thing

Joseph Milford might just be the Philippe Petit of contemporary American poetry. His Tattered Scrolls and Postulates shows us nothing less than an ingeniously shaped poetic imagination and a seemingly inexhaustible supply of astonishing lines. These new poems are rich with pathos, wisecracks, jeremiads, allusions, and invocations; they're like fractured sonnets whose dare is to get as many turns in as possible. In the dizzying world of the twenty-four-hour news cycle and ubiquitous social media, he provides us with an equally unnerving but wholly lyrical alternative.

Michael Tyrell, author of The Wanted and Phantom Laundry

Joe Milford knows things that are reserved for true artists and the sainted mad. He spills them in torrents of fire. Joe claims to be knee-deep in the unsayable. Maybe so, but he does a damned fine job of pushing through the scars of the wounded world and reports back to us in language imbued with light. Truth lives in these tattered scrolls and postulates and you would do well to listen. Joe's got the goods.

Jeff Weddle, Eudora Welty Prize winning author of Bohemian New Orleans: The Story of the Outsider and Loujon Press.

Tattered Scrolls and Postulates, Joseph Milford's striking sequence, transports us to a bizarre neighborhood where "every elevator is a minefield" and the famous castaway "Alexander Selkirk sleeps in a tent in my backyard and befriends neighbors and stray dogs." As the title of his book suggests, Milford is quite content to mingle the ancient with the futuristic and all that falls between. He demonstrates how an epic work may emerge from an ambitious series of short poems, each standing alone yet connected one to the other. His enormous and agile imagination takes in "aphelion, apogee, ascending node" alongside an "armadillo carcass," as well as "Jesse James," "Grunewald's Crucifixion," "biplanes," "butterflies," and "bad-ass tats." It represents a truly American vision in its openness, its frankness, its wildly divergent energies, and its sheer blood-and-guts grandeur, a true bag of infinite holding, in which Milford unapologetically acknowledges "I will never kill a beautiful mythic beast for you" yet reassuring in a friendly tone that you can always call "if you need anything."

Ernest Hilbert, author of Sixty Sonnets and All of You on the Good Earth

A Happy Meal of a poem! Wake up Walt Whitman, there's a new kid trespassing on the grass -
I think you'll like him.

Leonard Gontarek, author of Déjà vu Diner and He Looked Beyond My Faults And Saw My Deeds

The first time I was in a fist fight was, in no way, similar to the clean, choreographed bouts seen in movies or TV shows. Despite the noble adolescent goal of standing up for myself, what ensued was a chaotic flurry of fists and feet in a cloud of dust. Once it was over, though, the adrenaline continued to course through my veins, and I was compelled to recast the story to all my friends in epic terms. Reading Tattered Scrolls and Postulates was a similar experience for me, albeit less bloody. Milford uses lines of poetry the way Bruce Lee used nunchakus, yet in the aggregate they evoke Dante or Milton. His speaker is in a life-or-death confrontation with the mundane, at times offering the lucid observations of a thoughtful, middle-aged working man, at other times the relentless, kaleidoscopic ragings of a soul in solitary confinement. In a punk-rock-paced Odyssean quest through the steady noise of work-a-day American life, Tattered Scrolls and Postulates brings together the verbal carnival ride of Dean Young with the allusion-filled breadth and epic depth of Eliot's "The Wasteland". It's an exciting, troubling, and edifying read.

Alx Johns is an Associate Professor of English at the University of North Georgia, recipient of the 2013 Pavement Saw Press Chapbook Prize for "Robot Cosmetics," and the managing director of Athens Word of Mouth, a monthly reading series bringing together nationally known and local writers.

Joe Milford has lived a life devoted to modern poetry. With this most recent collection he has skillfully combined classical themes with accessible language. Known around literary circles for his long running radio program, Milford's greatest literary gift has always been giving, and here he has given his readers an awful lot to think about.

John Dorsey, author of Shoot the Messenger

Table of Contents

Primordial Vesicle

So that we come to know we all migrate into putrid and wanton gestation.
So that we come to know the cruciform as only one notch in the ancient always tree.
So that we come to know that our constellation is made without our permission.
So that we come to know that we must document those stars and how we orbit them.
So that we come to know we are turds eating turds in carbon cyclic composition.
So that we come to know our cave-vulva birthburn into flesh-layered pupa.
So that we come to know that great eels and worms crawl our DNA pulsating.
So that we come to know that we are cleansed through fire not water through salt and sulphur.
So that we come to know the brain is a jellyfish anthive spore-filled landfill of looms.
So that we come to know that the afterlife's roots taste like the hell's tongues of dribbling whores.

...

So that we come to know medusae ganglia writhe our sargassic morphic fields' hunt of Artemis.
So that we come to know that we host hosts of imposters and truths in our cellular structures.
So that we come to know there is no afterlife only everlife its forms always violent animals.
So that we come to know this grit spun about the collider will find godparticle or slag-colander.
So that we come to know our journal is but flesh of word interrupted by crucifixions.
So that we never forget that the grotesque is the stickman being cracked open to ooze its stories.
So that we never forget our keys before descending into the belly of the thousand coiled ears.
So that we never forget our gelatinous self before the bones made us forget how

to transmute.
So that we never forget the garden of earthly delights as we ride the subway langlinguage.
So that we never forget we appear to each other's souls as something covered in Vaseline.

. . .

So that we never forget chess is only how you stagger through the Mayan soccer deathgame.
So that we never forget we make our larvae the soft crutches for ideas of acid and lye.
So that we never forget minions talk us up as they suck as down into the arid vortex of fuck.
So that we never forget that language was held in a skull like blood and was spilled at our birth.
So that we never forget the mandolin heard when we left our bodies and the trombone entered.
So that we never forget joist and jest lathe and lust fester and foist and brutal love and crystal.
So that we never forget we ride the great steed and are the great steed simultaneously brethren.
So that we never forget many wings touching the top of the cave while guano made museums.
So that we never forget that the jaguar eats us while birthing us the blood on its canines is us.
So that we never forget caliphate infidel tongue versus wombmouth with hungry ghosts hovering.

. . .

A kaleidoscopic weave allowing poet to merge with Rimbaud as homunculus-voice from abyss.
A kaleidoscopic weave allowing American steaming fast-food bowels to lacerate and be emptied.
A kaleidoscopic weave writhing up ancient totem phallus exchanging primal vesicle bion orgon.
A kaleidoscopic weave of vegetable, animal, human, mineral, celestial, chthonic, astral intelligences.
A kaleidoscopic weave of quetzal, jaguar, bison, swordfish, seahorse, all burning

to bone nautilus.

A kaleidoscopic weave in the core where Kali dances and the black goddess maze of vulva pulses.

A kaleidoscopic weave of sutra and mandala all of us omen-makers our invisible Anubis-helmets.

A kaleidoscopic weave through a Breughelian landscape populated by bird-headed men harvesting.

A kaleidoscopic weave where we pull the veil back drink from the wound in Ourobouros scales.

A kaleidoscopic weave into which we spelunk infinitely reading the cave-walls of the spiral.

...

A kaleidoscopic weave to escape UFO abduction fear which is only visitation of our past animals.

A kaleidoscopic weave helping the reptile cortex fuck the mammal cortex to birth human pigment.

A kaleidoscopic weave of fin antler hand scale feather leaf spine talon flipper wing tongue finger.

A kaleidoscopic weave of fortress tetrahedron geode triquetra lemniscate vortices rapidly mutating.

A kaleidoscopic weave of your grindstone my anvil your decanter my alembic this apothecary.

...

"There is no route out of the maze. The maze shifts as you move through it, because it is alive."

Philip K. Dick, VALIS

•

"Much evidence indicates that the person least likely to receive information via paranormal routes is a man who enjoyed a generally happy childhood, who is not a twin, and who comes from a family with no interest or belief in the paranormal. Predictors to particular sensitivity to psi are:

1) coming from a family with a history of psi and/or where psychic powers are accepted as a fact of life;

2) being a child of multiple birth, e.g., a twin or triplet, and

3) suffering serious trauma in one's first 10-12 years of life. Two frequent sources of trauma are living in a home where one or more adults are alcoholics and living with a habitually angry and abusive parent. Especially gifted psychics have experienced more than one of the above circumstances."

Sylvia Hart Wright, "Childhood Influences That Heighten Psychic Powers", Journal of Spirituality and Paranormal Studies

•

"So if you ever get down where the black trees grow
And meet a voodoo lady named Marie Laveau
If she ever asks you to make her your wife
Man, you better stay with her for the rest of your life"

Bobby Bare lyrics, "Marie Laveau"

"A man sets out to draw the world. As the years go by, he peoples a space with images of provinces, kingdoms, mountains, bays, ships, islands, fishes, rooms, instruments, stars, horses, and individuals. A short time before he dies, he discovers that the patient labyrinth of lines traces the lineaments of his own face."

Jorge Luis Borges, The Aleph and Other Stories

•

"In the solitude resounding
Distant footsteps echo free.
Is it thou who flamest, bounding
Circles of infinity?"

Alexander Blok, "Into Crimson Dark"

•

"The devil's ascended
Upon some crystal wings
In the citadel lightning
Splits a cloud of butterflies and fiends
And with a vacant stare, I'll leave a flower there"

Mark Lanegan lyrics, "Harborview Hospital"

Tattered Scrolls and Postulates: Volume I

Poems, Viscera, Encyclopedia, Esoterica

1.

i wanted the specific procedure to bleed the TV sitcom families out of me.
vendettas spill over verandas and fertilize the gardens. ivies and vines asplendor.
we hovel in the garrison under a curse of ancient portents. Disillusion—our raiment.
the papyri were shredded to light the kindling. the spires of fires conspiring.
things were more insidious than asbestos lingering in our catacombs.
the entire population was just a few French fries short of a Happy Meal.
the ghosts of books read find slippage under the screen door into the grass to fume.
the stagecraft was amazing as the postcards shot through the crowd maiming all of us.
a mystery creature comes to you with a set of keys. you ask which door. it gnashes its teeth.
there is no power-source for the great apparatus. we still hung from the giant killswitch.

Notes

Happy Meals are boxed meals created by MacDonald's food chain in 1979—they are
marketed towards children and usually use a tie-in with a movie or television program in
order to cross-promote with a toy or game included with the meal. The meal comes with
a burger, fries, a cookie, and a drink. In my idiom, being "a few French fries short of a
Happy Meal" means that you aren't quite right in the head.

2.

one can never have enough LEGOS during a mid-life crisis; this is the slow cure for Alzheimer's.
they kept saying my future was held in my hands' palms. i sliced that future up with farmwork.
i can smell the musk, the scat, the sulphur, the burnt metals and plastics of a poem passing by.
like that warty sphere on the counter about to become a gourd to be hollowed out for a birdnest.
i remember diving off of Lover's Leap and hoping to die but came out the other diabolical portal.
i remember that a fatal shot to the heart was the killswitch but i came out like sideways bullets.
if you ever see a kid standing in golden wheat or goldenrod—rescue him. truly, America kills.
i am made of tusks covered in leather. i move like a clay golem throughout religions. dream me.
some pop-songs are so covered in suntan lotion that i remember my sharkbites. ah, spring break.
on a white piece of construction paper, my stepdaughter killed my ninjas. it hurt nanoseconds.

Notes

LEGOS are multi-faceted construction and imagination tools developed by The Lego
Group in Bilund, Denmark since 1949. Alzheimer's is a form of dementia which
affects thought processes and memory—there are some theories which suggest that this
condition can be addressed or improved with creative and analytical exercises. Lover's
Leap—there are many of these locations, which all share a high altitude and a history of
purposeful, suicidal jumps related to romantic tragedies. I am referring to the one at De
Soto Caverns, Alabama. Catcher in the Rye—the idea of "catching children" in this stanza
is a direct reference to the novel by J.D. Salinger. Golem—a golem is a magical creature,
typical to Jewish legends and folklore, created through arcane methods from inanimate
mater—wood, clay, stone, metal, etc.

3.

if you paint a garden and do not like the branch then finish the painting and grab a ladder & saw.
the morphic field altered by language is a word or series of words you must covet like a badge.
your father's shadow always eclipsed the sundial's, so you never knew what damn time it was.
always thought i'd like to have a Jesuit education but never would want a Jesuit congregation.
one must always attain a maximum intensity with a minimum of means said Miro the bullfighter.
a red fox implanted with her RFID chip saunters constantly around our house stealing identities.
how does one separate the dust from anything he or she has done; how does one leave this earth?
amoebic vehicles harvest skeletal and biological permutations amongst an ocean of germinations.
without dirt there would be no clouds. without hammocks there would be no drunks. kick dust.
as kids we had honeysuckle, crab-apples, grounded pecans, muscadines, sour-grass—all aplenty.

Notes

Morphic fields—a morphic field is a theoretical idea that there are fields, much like quantum fields in physics, which react and organize in order to establish specific cellular patterns in plants, animals, bacteria, etc. In other words, morphic fields decide whether cells will become kidneys or fingers, even though all cells seem to be programmed identically. Miro the bullfighter—this is a reference to Joan Miro's painting, The Matador. RFID chips—these radio frequency devices can be attached to things or implanted into them in order to track information using electromagnetic fields. Muscadines are a grape-like vine species found in the south of North America. Muscadine wine is particularly dangerous.

4.

the ash falling was the closest thing to snowfall this hellpocket was ever going to be blessed with.
it was tenebrous to say the least and it was in the abates and we loathed a coming ritual solstice.
you were always drunk at other men's weddings and never sober at their funerals and a virgin.
there are no inhospitable islands to vanquish sinners on. they become convenience store cashiers.
as we spread lime for next year's tomatoes, the world writhed in endless top ten lists. cuckolds.
crawdads circling like an underwater zodiac as i unhook the catfish from my chickenwire lures.
Ascletario was eaten by dogs when he should have been burned. O, the stars, the stars, the stars.
had i been named Cadillac Williams, not a Protestant Irish moniker, what could have happened?
sea urchins thriving about the planet like the halitosis of your hangover and dust of bad checks.
Algol mer. 6:25 ev. Moon Leo. 35 degrees N. Lat 75 degrees. Long. Sun sets at 5:28. days too short.

Notes

I assume the reader knows what crawdads are? Ascletario was an ancient Roman astrologer
in the time of Titus. Algol (coordinates)—the line beginning with Algol (a bright star
in the Pegasus constellation) is a set of coordinates and astrological information for a
particular day. Algol is also a demon associated with this star who apparently is prominent
on Halloween.

5.

i built a circle of wolves around our lot and kept the house transparent so our children learned.
do you know how blurred your lenses have become? that's why pilots' goggles are your fetish.
integers, increments, wreathes and cockles' coils. staple walls for nothing. corrosive grease boils.
satyrs run as far as they can and then the rain forests are burned down and dire men hunt them.
ancient DNA abacus spirals back to the mitochondria and waits for a mate to make me perfect.
i was his liver. vultures ate me every day. he would carry me into the office. that terrible display.
i was given a stone by a man and the man said a man was contained within the stone. i threw it.
coyote, with your jowls chaffed, we will feed you. come to the sliding glass doors. eat. lick lips.
i saw all scarecrows dismount and lunge in a hurricane towards Promised Land and Neverland.
stop glimmering—the moths kinetic flock to you—i can't penetrate their shifting webs of wings.

Notes

Mitochondria are found in the eukaryotic cells which compose most life on this planet.
Prometheus was a Greek god notorious for giving mankind fire and knowledge. The
Jewish Promised Land—this was the land promised to Abraham, Isaac, and Jacob by
the Hebrew God, and it was to exist between the River of Egypt and the Euphrates.
Neverland—the fantasy dwelling of Peter Pan and the Lost Boys.

6.

held up by the neck as whelps in some terrible blinding light and they checked us for adequacy.
when the only three vehicles left at your disposal are the taxicab, ambulance, or squad car.
pockmarked with geysers stricken with bullet-holes. viscous with ampules. you in the hallway.
i was tossed like a chewed bone. left not for dead but for life to find my marrow. to suckle it.
millet grist powder silt resin for the words to imbue with lustre liquid and molten tongue-blood.
and though poetry was a planet of obsidian onyx ice we chipped sharp sherds from it to fling.
trolling deep in undercurrent, evil fish, a light hangs from its spine to let it see what it must eat.
the time i spent scraping at my bar-code, at my UPC, i should have spent escaping commodity.
i scrawled your voodoo names and secret words onto wooden pine knots. they in the coffee can.
phase 1: specimen. phase 2: study of specimens. phase 3: hunt them. phase 4: free the specimens.

Notes

Lantern fish are anglerfish who sometimes grow "lanterns" from their foreheads, organs which are bioluminescent for hunting in the deep dark. UPC stands for "Universal Product Code", a symbolic method of tracking items and products for sale.

7.

which instrument to play in the valley, on the cliffs, by the ocean, underwater, in the last coffin?
i was stoned out of my gourd through high school but that did not deter the 9-headed hydra.
would you believe me that the Gates to the Ardent World are can openers, Q-Tips, thumbtacks?
in the bucket, down the well, with pendulum, reciting the names of all the saints you had known.
the prom queen is running from the angry swan & the record-spinner is coked-up. summertime.
covered myself in roadkill & laid in the green field watching them circle closer and closer. slowly.
when you scream the moray eel jets out the killer bee lauches forth. rank mustard gas permeates.
your gutturals call language up from earth and your trills call language down from the grey sky.
i wanted the woman inside my mom's oil lamp–her trapped behind the oil beads on their wires.
all of writing is the robbing of graves. ancient owl stares you down the gun-barrel of oak branch.

Notes

The Hydra is the nine-headed mythic beast, from Greek mythology, defeated by Hercules at Lake Lerna. "Ardent World" is a skin-care and cosmetic product company in the Phillipines, but, for me, it is an imaginary symbolic world where everything is burning with idyllic passion—yet another false utopia.

8.

after 1000's of years of losing our sharkteeth against glass, we finally cut through the aquarium.
too many candles in the trees too many Christmas lights over the ponds too many barren angels.
the deer keep leaping into the onslaught of metal misconstruing it as a river attempting to dowse.
flurries came through the homestead and i took the scalpel and opened my chest to melt them all.
i collected priceless calamities—tried to keep them in attic Swisher Sweet boxes, but they melted.
i was inside the whiskey bottle where no one could hear screaming and he threw it shattering me.
if we could have an orchard of orchids and fly through it like ghosts i'd sign that lease and deed.
my mom thought it was a great idea us sunburned picking strawberries in baskets for stepfather.
in this flooded and dead Georgia, i wonder where the snakes have all gone. makes me nervous.
moon shining on the shovel and then i knew i should not be here. i am knee-deep in unsayable.

Notes

Swisher Sweets are a namebrand of flavored tobacco products which sometimes come in wooden boxes imbued with the smell of the flavor of the cigars or cigarettes.

9.

gliders flew over the graveyards and forests and landed on our lawns with letters of reliquaries.
she is on the phone and i see her genuflecting and know it is a man who may or may not pay her.
a sharp shrapnel dancer spun about my cuts and made a beard for me of stained church-glass.
glimpses is all they are; water-striders speed across cold Tennessee eyeball inlet over blue stones.
your pipe has not yet changed many colors. come here more often. recline back porch by woods.
that time on the phone i saw the gray squirrel killed by car while talking of the Marvin Bell poem.
inside the ancient dresser from the flea market i found a copy of Francis Bacon from old library.
everyone keeps asking about what i am using the woodshed for out back and i can't really say.
young whelps skinning the last sheen off the hardwood floors with their birthday scamperings.
tight ivy wrapped most of our stories, so they had to be loosened with a longlasting campfire.
i don't have to be Wiccan to know the solstice and the equinox; i have the Farmer's Almanac.

Notes

Water-striders, also known as gerrids, are a species of spiders or bugs which have the ability to shift their weight in order to walk on water. Marvin Bell is an esteemed poet, the writer of the Dead Man poems, and was once my teacher at the University of Iowa. The Farmer's Almanac is a publication, since 1792, which has "spoken to all walks of life: tide tables for those who live near the ocean; sunrise and planting charts for those who live on the farm; recipes for those who live in the kitchen; and forecasts for those who don't like the question of weather left up in the air." Francis Bacon was a 16th and 17th century philosopher and scientist who is also called the "father of Empiricism". A Wiccan is a person who practices Wicca or the practice of modern-day paganism and nature worship.

10.

i never said astronaut when asked about growing up--never said fireman either. said smuggler.
most horses won't jump an abyss or another dead horse. horses won't jump a saddle. omens.
hematite dark shadows across the lawn the oaks whistling with Palmetto bugs big as thumbs.
they said the idiot savant in Coralville could read the voices of stones better than meteorologists.
our conversation was epically punctuated in the storm by the broken wiper and rickety cadence.
the god of backyards emerged from the creek with orange cap and fish-hooks hanging all over.
i said i am sick of it and my friend said over the phone that he has the lime bags and the shovel.
like a buck sharpening antlers on trees, we sharpen ourselves on lawmen and women. golden.
the world is indigo but we pretend it is pink. i hate those who sell media purple to the ignorant.
sometimes one's life is a bitching wife in a parking lot and in the adjacent car is the sweet one.

Notes

Hematite is a product of iron ore which is usually black or silver-grey. Palmetto Bugs
are huge cockroaches associated with damp climates and the Southern United States.
Coralville is a town, near Iowa City, IA, full of mystics.

11.

most times the uranium canyon can't be mined and the suburbs suffer like slave-regimes.
at the crossroads where one discerns what to scuttle, what to buttress, what heaven to lean to.
what shadow-work is this? giant whales of fog spilling krill of dew across the barren cowfields.
he said godspeed and you gave such a look of disdain to him that the church doors flew open.
moss, lichen, soft turf—the hands of dark forests encroaching and no fires can hold them back.
he sat in front of the Dollar Store chewing tobacco with fire ants crawling up his prosthetic leg.
dogs divvying up territories between the two churches, the Freemasons' lodge, the firehouse.
at grandpa Joe's, you best be careful what you wish for before opening woodshop coffee cans.
in the old warehouse were hundreds of frames of all sizes and we imagined paintings for each.
you kept the Iowa snowball in a cooler and drove it to Georgia. i covered it with syrup. ate it.

Notes

Uranium mining is accomplished through various chemical and technical processes in order to procure the element for nuclear power generation—a common side effect of exposure to these processes is terminal lung cancer among miners and nearby populations if the mining clean-up is not done properly. Grandpa Joe is a mythic figure in this book you are reading and is based upon my real fraternal grandfather, Joe Milford, whose namesake I inherited.

12.

giant plastic tub of beef jerky on the counter as cashier talks about seeing Tom Petty live once.
burning sage over the burned down house seemed strange to me but she said it must need be.
in the closet, old ruddy bespeckled arms began to extend from the sleeves of shirts and jackets.
between two powerlines on the left side of the road the huge spiderwebs proudly glistened.
i could kill someone with innocence and i could introduce violence. this is how fruits ripen.
deprive everything of oxygen. watch the world panic. deprive everything of Christmas lights.
i inherited Lucregia Borgia. shot it until the muzzle melted and destroyed a national treasure.
evil squaw of a neighbor called animal control on us. we adorned the bottle tree for protection.
in the woods behind the homestead the mound of the old railroad wound like a serpent-god.
the bleached dog's skull rests atop the occult text on the black poetry bookshelf, a black tower.

Notes

Tom Petty is an American blues and rock and roll popular music icon. Lucretia Borgia
is the fond nickname of Buffalo Bill's .50 caliber trapdoor needle gun. "Squaw" is the
(mainly derogatory) term for a Native American female, most likely originating with
the Massachusetts Algonquin tribe. Serpent-gods—this is a reference to any number
of reptilian gods, such as the Nagas, Apop, Quetzacoatl, etc., who permeate all ancient
cultures of the world. "Burning Sage" is a custom which is used to cleanse one's home of
evil spirits—it does not always work. A bottle-tree is any tree adorned with empty bottles
upon branches—they ward off evil spirits—for example, my mother thought a witch
lived next to her, and so she put bottles on the branches of the tree between their two
yards.

13.

the geeps and shoats chewed through the fence and got into traffic causing a major pile-up.
glass windchimes breaking the lights while they pulse sounds and rainbows littered his porch.
they kept calling him a national treasure but he drank whiskey and puked lobster on the mayor.
first vertebra of your neck which holds up the head is called the atlas mine; it is hairline cracked.
in the attic was a chair by the window, a toy gun in the dust on the floor beside it. rat pellets. loss.
the water moccasins broiled out of the black pond parting wet leaves after i threw the rock there.
i think of Boccioni, of Futurism, while buying cole slaw and batteries. hot check-out girl Lateshia.
the quest for the golden fleece always obvious while flipping burgers and skimming the register.
pecan groves and their symmetries golden down the longitudes towards long-fading antebellum.
gathering kindling when i hear the shift in the cooler, ice melting, beer cans slushing. hurry up.

Notes

Geeps, shoats—a geep is a genetic chimera of a sheep and a goat; a shoat is a newly
weaned baby pig. Umberto Boccioni was an Italian painter and sculptor who helped
to shape the Futurism movement. Futurism is a movement of 20th century Italian art
concerned with aeroplanes, trains, cars, etc. and the progressive violence of speed and
technology. The Golden Fleece was the wool of the Colchis Ram quested for by Jason and
the Argonauts. Water moccasins are prominent poisonous snakes in Georgia, also known
as cottonmouths.

14.

i was full of ergophobia whittling mermaids from cedar and balsa on a porch amidst the cosmos.
we lost the leavining, sold out the reckoning; we wished for prudence and gave away to sea salt.
i have found that writing in the morning makes the herb garden flourish. i have found salience.
most of the evil of this place was the fact it was once an ocean. Appalachian chains underwater.
landlord calls from his deerstand to check in. the heating unit died. saw my breath in the kitchen.
telemetry made this possible. shrooms made this possible. skunk brew made this possible. alms.
all you had to know about murder was that the wedding ring was found atop the compost heap.
red Georgia clay like the flesh of the earth asking me to make men and women from it. O glory.
my grandpa called them laundry bags. his parachutes over Germany with artillery. good man.
they found something unspeakable in a cave near my home. the government showed up. damn.

Notes

Ergophobia is the fear of finding a job. Telemetry is the automated communications process by which measurements are made and other data collected at remote or inaccessible points and transmitted to receiving equipment for monitoring. The Appalachian Mountain chain was once underwater—you can find seashells on its peaks. When I refer to shrooms in this text, unless otherwise noted, I mean the psychedelic kind.

15.

it really is a good option that this entire species should die with no record of it. entertain this.
i loaded a cannon with peach-pits, a shotgun with peanut shells, a pistol with a cherry seeds.
i always thought i could lash anything together to stop the bleeding of the world. idealist.
cairn and crib. corn in the fridge. holidays and their bagpipes. tensions in the hovel. wreaths.
when i think of dragons i think of koi and how they live in my underbrain in meningal soup.
in the winter, as we drive parcels home, i can see all the nests in trees now. makes me happy.
what does it mean for the panopticon to shred its Tarot cards into your hands like canopy rain?
you can eat snout. you can eat hoof. you can eat jowl. you can eat guts. you can eat memories.
like a spider that makes its underwater web i think i should kiss you in a bubble. a trap-whisper.
in the blue mist of the morning i cleaned sleep from my eyes and a slingstone cut my cheekbone.

Notes

The Tarot refers to any number of divination methods using highly ornate cards with images on them; in the Major Arcana, for instance, you wil find cards such as The Hanged Man, The Fool, The Devil, The Tower, the Wheel of Fortune, etc. Underwater spiders, or "diving-bell spiders", are a species of Arachnids who live their whole lives underwater. A panopticon is a building, like a prison or hospital, built so that all of its interior can be viewed from a single point. Koi are wonderfully colored carp which people domesticate because of their ornamental appearance.

16.

when you throw a sharp object into the air, those who do not run are historians. others, soldiers.
Saint Augustine, the stars were signifiers, a language—not causes, not predictors. i gaze up.
the fingerprints on the pine shovel handle make wheels that augurs have lost the arts to read.
i swallowed an octopus to make a wheel around my heart but bad voodoo made me bait caught.
it has been a long time in this parish of churches that anyone has met a true cleric. birds wait too.
no great ship or galleon could ever sail the creek of my imagination in that graveyard backyard.
ending my days as a Baptist, they tar and feather me with locusts and honey. a honeycomb deity.
i learned that plagiarism was history before the 7th century. before that too. give me Happy Meal.
bract and catkin, node and rhizome, floret and tuber--we take our baskets out in the goldswollen.
Ray Bradbury's books litter the shag carpet; i worry about the fate of Mars within wood paneling.

Notes

St. Augustine was a theologian and philosopher, heavily influenced by Manicheanism and
the Neo-Platonics, who helped shape Western Christianity and Catholocism. Tarred and
feathered refers to a punishment, usually in public for humiliation, where an individual
is covered with hot tar and then sprinkled or rolled in feathers—this is a highly painful
method of "justice". Ray Bradbury is an American mystery, science fiction, fantasy,
and horror writer. Augurs are seers who can see the future using a variety of divination
methods. Locusts and honey is a reference to John the Baptist. In my personal lexicon or
mindscape, octopi are symbols of ctuhllian influences, and to ingest them, to me, is to
communicate with the supernatural or occult—figuratively, literally, or poetically.

17.

i decided to devour. you wait for hours for your hero. i decided to eat a century. wipe my lips.
every elevator is a minefield—don't ask people which floor—they will spray blood everywhere.
stolid millennia, styrofoam will meet you--don't worry--those packing peanuts are in the crib.
walked out my house to find the entire neighborhood covered in cellophane then back inside.
we broke free from our Amsterdam fantasies to fall through glass walls under antique desks.
when you kill the Big Boss you get to advance to the next level when you kill the Big Boss you get
to advance to the next level; you must traverse the oil-black snowstorm until it's as white as flour.
shot through hamster tubes pneumatic trachea to zigzag towards the manhole out onto the street.
i'll never forget that time I conquered Carthage. that was one helluva damn riot-strewn weekend.
the thing about the old basement apartment—the windows would never open—succubi hovered.

Notes

Styrofoam is a manufactured polystyrene used in countless applications. Carthage was an
ancient Punic city once conquered by Hannibal and then later by the Roman Empire.
Succubi are female demons who supposedly have sex with dreaming or sleeping men. "Big
Boss" is a slang term in gaming for the monster or adversary you must kill to advance to
the next level of a video game.

18.

i almost died one morning making the bread apron string caught in mixer-arm semolina flying.
stagger in concentric circles a three-legged dog in a traffic frenzy; make it to the alley; meander.
exercise of pathos on paper keeps less Baalzebub out of the cabinets and closets less haunted.
he took his cowboy hat off and Universal Studios'film catalog all played at once. mesmerizing.
every dollar is a key to something else. all the doors of the greatest buildings. they wait for bills.
i saw a kid flip a swingset once. kept slinging himself into broken arms. after that, i is cautious.
plastic black mouse at my hand distorts the timespan of the scarab pushing its daily dungball.
by the magnolia i asked him how he did that morning he said nothing—buck too young to hit.
the Freemasons across the highway meet on Tuesdays—i notice and drink Pabst Blue Ribbon.
every night i'd come home stinkoed to that spooky portrait of that ancient matron by the stairs.

Notes

Semolina is a coarse wheat product used in couscous and breads. Baalzebub, or the
"Lord of the Flies", was also known as "The Prince of Demons" and was only outranked
by Satan in Pandemonium. Egyptian scarab myths derived from the scarab beetle who
would roll dungballs across the desert which, to the ancient Egyptians, was a symbolic
representation of the rising of the sun and the passage of time. Pabst Blue Ribbon is an
American beer associated with indie rockers and blue-collar workers. The Freemasons are
a fraternal society, mired in conspiracy, which this book references frequently.

19.

i found it ironic that the blood drive van was outside of the voting booths with its orange juice.
there are no more ice cream trucks in our neighborhood and cameras mount the telephone poles.
i remember bagging groceries at twelve at the Sav-U-Foods which became the Piggly Wiggly.
he was cursed to find every stoplight on the way home his face lit red as he cursed his moments.
how can i vibrate with intensity in this poor model; how can i realize my potential as a mere blip?
while i glorified human cruelty, in all of my decisions, i always prefered the wooden splinter.
the inch thick rot grubs like angry fingers writhed from the Augean Stables and the foul vomit.
i bounce checks across several counties for cheap beer and baby food. pay fees. write much more.
we studied The Iliad while the horses were sickened and our mothers slept in the crawlspaces.
orpiment can be cut by a knife, a fool's dust. goes to hot springs but knows it disintegrates fast.

Notes

Many readers will remember running out to the ice cream truck when you heard its music
fill your neighborhood. Piggly Wiggly was the first full service grocery store in America
founded in Memphis, Tennessee in 1916—it was also the first place I was ever employed
at the age of twelve with a work permit. Augean stables had to be cleaned by Hercules
as his fifth labor. The Iliad was the epic, credited to Homer, which told the story of the
Trojan War. Orpiment is a mineral used in artist's paints.

20.

no pandas are allowed in these poems. only koalas. no imperialism. no oriental. only koalas.
go south to find the bark of the cinchona tree to kill the fever and pox. i recommend it highly.
the shylocks reap a havest of forclosures down these two-lane highways, the for-sale signs.
Harpocrates waves his hands across the dark Georgia night silencing the crickets in the eaves.
procrustean fields, procrustean hours, procrustean phrases—cutting and pasting—excrutiating.
Dan McGrew and Stagolee hang out at the Tin Roof drinking rye and cleaning their rusty guns.
the actions of a wolf can be predicted by a full moon upon a copper sundial in a pine clearing.
make a wild sarsaparilla wash to cleanse your shingles—you can make a poultice. chew roots.
He is "the hard, energetic, horse-trading type of man who was remorsely indicated for survival."
her bra on the hardwood kitchen floor and the plastic dolphin toy as the 20-month old snores.

Notes

The Cinchona tree's bark has medicinal purposes and has been used by the Peruvians
for centuries—the Jesuits popularized it in Europe, and it was used in the treatment
of malaria and a source for quinine. Shylock is a slang term for loan shark derived
from Shakespeare's character in The Merchant of Venice. Harpocrates is the Greek god
of silence. "Procrustean", in this poem, refers to the ancient Attican blacksmith who
would cut people's legs off to make their bodies fit his iron beds. Dan McGrew was
a legendary prospector popularized in a poem by Robert Service. Stagolee ("Stagger
Lee") was a legendary pimp popularized in many songs recorded by the likes of The
Clash, Mississippi John Hurt, Woody Guthrie, and James Brown, just to name a few.
Sarsaparilla was once a popular soft drink, like root beer, in the American wild west.

21.

On The Explanation That The Body Of The World Cannot Possibly Be Infinite. On Mirrors That Burn.
and so i live in Erewhon looking for more educated Yahoos. waiting centuries for them. sombre.
there are fewer Whitmans in the 21st century. look to me. i might be an adequate singer of selves.
my first word was scone. orphanage, i suppose. my next word was window. it all makes sense.
before my first haircut, my hair was bluegrass. after that, i think vines grew like Charlie Daniels.
whosoever shall compel thee to go a mile, go with him for twain. we colleagues pick our brains.
i can't stand old whore vultures with pagan medallions and fake tits & droolings at readings.
Fauvists knew that the argument was over color, as in which color do you see while you die?
fishing with bamboo rod. silk line. hook made from bone or needle. leftover fried rice as bait.
i love my hoodie hung on random nail because the ghost of D.A. Levy is coming over tonight.

Notes

On The Explanation That The Body Of The World Cannot Be Infinite and On Mirrors
That Burn are two esoteric texts either real or invented. Erewhon is a fantasy world, which
satirizes Victorian society, created by Samuel Butler. The Yahoos were brutish creatures
found in Jonathon Swift's Gulliver's Travels. Walt Whitman was the American poet who
authored Leaves of Grass. Charlie Daniels is an American country-Western musician
popular for the song "The Devil Went Down To Georgia". The Fauvists were a post-
Impresionist group of French artists, led initially by Matisse, who approached nature with
bold brushstrokes and techniques, such as painting directly out of the paint tubes. D.A.
Levy was an underground poet and indie publisher mainly residing in Cleveland who
passed in 1968.

22.

cannonballs through bass-lines twist my guts into better knots that no bullet could pierce.
end loop. dropper loop. bowline. figure eight. clove hitch. end loop 1. end loop 2. end loop 3.
you can only drag so many skulls behind you before you have to make a grand metropolis.
necropolis leaves its skulls to calcify. great cities of the soil. skull-holder, plant bulbous seeds.
he crawled out of the coma in the deer carcass and a year later you could see antlers growing.
Alexander Selkirk sleeps in a tent in my backyard and befriends nosy neighbors and stray dogs.
things went agee. the wind was esse. we found ourselves trying to cage miniature tornadoes.
Fomalhaut rises 4:31am. Algorab meridian to come. Shaula rises as well. Procyon sets 10:41pm.
i count how many carwrecks i have had and compare those to the fact i ever occurred. wrecker.
i would love to fly to the moon. but i can't. actually i could actually. still, i like my sawdust life.

Notes

Maritime knots are mentioned in the second line of this poem. Alexander Selkirk was
a Scottish sailor who was marooned on a desert island for four years and became the
inspiration for Daniel Dafoe's Robinson Crusoe. Fomalhaut, Algorab, Shaula, Procyon,
etc. are astrological chart references.

23.

opened stables and cleaned them as Hercules. there were rot grubs bigger than wrestlers' fingers.
played guitars so hard strings ran from me—women said i'd never be a man until i played a harp.
i was so nervous—instead of butterflies i've got frogs. i had short arms and deep deep pockets.
the electroplate technique for ormolu is not too hard to perfect in a properly equipped shed.
the path integral within the canonical S-matrix primarily will make Wick's expansion gleeful?
parking cars on Indian burial grounds which are actually Cherokee cursed—our supreme courts.
i hate when wind makes me lose my chain of thought. i actually then chain wind and chastise it.
do sharks crave light so much that they wait for the blood from the sun to fill their black eyes?
when someone gambles, his face changes—incredulous morphs & mutations. loud as hell mutes.
i thought she was behind me. she may have left forever. parakeets in cages. me with empty pens.

Notes

Hercules, of course, was the half-immortal son of Zeus, popularized by his Twelve Labors, and a life of tragedy, from Greek mythology. Ormolu is gold or brass used for decorative purposes, typically on furniture, or in my experience, on frames. S-Matrix theory in quantum physics is dynamic in approaching scattered or scattering effects—Heisenberg adored it. Gian-Carlo Wick was a quantum physiscist associated with Fermi's group who worked with theories of imaginary time. A Cherokee curse is particularly bad—the one I refer to is the North Carolina curse of the young brave, the uncle of Yo-na-gus-ka, who cursed General Rutherford and subsequent future "whites", as he died by a white oak after drinking from a sulphur stream.

24.

i found a cello of you in a cave and played as hard as i could and died and then you anteloped.
you made pottery when the empire burned. you burned fiddles under the cairn for the kiln.
i was swallowed whole by a whale-wasp. i asked if it was a god or goddess. it fucking laughed.
i had so many paths attached to me—like i was a broken sewing machine clogged with thread.
she walks by with a strategic strand of her hair dyed like a DNA braggard. she evolves upfront.
i killed all of my heroes. we were all Odysseus. listening to the same old gorgeous roaring oars.
no machines allowed. no humans. no seltzers. we coiled into new furs. we ignored all the stars.
being torn sideways is nicer than being torn wideways. they recover violence. a great pear grows.
most of us quit hoping. we ate value meals. a pegasus flew from a super-sized meal and brayed.
you pickle things. we all do. put the vagina in a jar with salt. a way of aborting fruits for men. eat.

Notes

The "whale-wasp" was an imaginary, and terrifying, monster that I imagined in a childhood nightmare. Odysseus was a warrior, king, vagabond, father, and husband returning home to his kingdom of Ithaca after the Trojan War (in Greek tales and literature). The Pegasus was a winged horse, whose name I use in the proper sense, as a verb, from Greek mythos.

25.

how many times will a judge snort his Scotch while a young hot woman knows his weak wife?
overheard a student say she could "suck a quarter out of a traffic meter"; walked back to office.
in the belly of the elephant was the birdcage in the cage was the fear of raptors and rodents.
a mite crawling along the spine of a feather would taste cat's blood later on whiskers of a dog.
SUV hemoglobin pumping corporates into urban organs cellphone calls in ballet around skylines.
mode on node off to annotate otherwise certification for the Promethean holograph mech-tech.
rain-splattered gazebo in parking lot students negotiate pot tempting K-9's and camera mounts.
falling through flipcharts into pixels down through molecules and bubbles the guts of crystals.
i had majic orca eyeball for oracle but dropped it in fryvat it sizzled prophecies in terrible rasps.
a green-spotted horned slug covered in slime glistening crawled over the opaque slug of lead.

Notes

Scotch is good for you if you don't overdo it—single malt, especially (which I've only had once or twice). K-9 Units are specially marked police vehicles who contain an officer and a trained dog, usually a German Shepherd, which has been trained to sniff out and detect any myriad kinds of contraband in your home or car. The Orcinus Orca is the terrifying killer whale.

26.

collapsing corrugations and jumping from vaporizing peaks they disentegrate into pulverizilles.
i had enough grease in my hair to get out of the ligatures and crawl to the canoe to tail you.
i once sprayed some lizards at my uncle's house in Florida with bugspray to watch them die.
dropped from high altitudes into deep waters to be spit from geysers and ride on the zephyrs.
interested as he was in secret pentagrams and circles he was easily and discreetly disposed of.
secret doors were under his tongue where languages lurked like virgins upon sacred grounds.
wild boar are not to be tampered with for death lurks here in Arcadia and the baby has a fever.
waiting for you is leaf in the drying cement during your parents' divorce it changes everything.
we wallow in this material instead of creating places for heavenly wallowings. of sleaze i sing.
a fearless core. we just want to be core. we are more like zucchini blosoms. we become fruitious.

Notes

Arcadia is a mythical land of legend in Greece and the home of Pan, a pastoral Greek god—the Latin phrase, "Et in Arcadia ego" is what I am referencing here—that death will eventually appear, or is always waiting, in what is otherwise a beautiful paradise or beautiful natural place.

27.

turkey vultures never cry. they harrow. shillings of rain on armadillo ribs. someone is doing community service in the hot GA sun. i have the robots to do it. i invested in those. i don't want to use them because of collateral damage. seriously, i have the robots. creatures in the carpet scaring me. i get further away as i get older. my child speaks to them. they exchange robots.
fried foods inside my body as i swim in the over-chlorinated pool. toxicity in the best ways. swallowing the most unearthly leisure. doing autoposies on live astronauts when they get back.
i think that pliers should be left out. i think in need of a class or two. no surgery for godsplinters.
what's mine is heirs. what's your usury? build obelisks that say:"he said the obelisk too much."
many times i asked to be abducted by aliens; did not get 1 anal probe? can't blame me for trying.
Magritte there when his mother was dragged out of the water; he was only 14. he starts painting.

Notes

Turkey vultures are huge raptors prominent in the American South who are often found eating roadkill and have a tough time taking off because of their mass. "Godsplinter" is a self-reference to a poem I once wrote, found in Cracked Altimeter, called "Godschrapnel", whose premise is that all of the forms in the universe are fragments of an exploded deity or consciousness. Magritte and his mother's death: Magritte's mother, after many attempts to commit suicide, finally succeeded in doing so when he was 13 years old—when they retrieved her corpse from the River Sambre, supposedly her dress was covering her face—this veil or suffocating image became a theme in Magritte's work.

28. a

no one does that themselves. if anyone wipes your tears, it is only because you have no arms,
until the equipment. others have done much worse. crackpipes in $35000 cars. i just snuck beers.
i can't beat Duchamp at chess. "I have come to the conclusion that while all chess players are artists,
not all artists are chess players"; it was extremely pleasurable to nekked type this.
i am more afraid of ghost sharks than real sharks. if you have seen a ghost shark, and you drop your
nail-file, then you know. the ghost sharks are the worst. they maim far constellations.
my sandcastle was made of severed arms. it was so sticky. i was covered with gore. when you are
covered with gore, and you are the quarterback, they clean you off real good. photo-ops ensue.
the entire universe tried to fit a bikini on the infinite. it came up with an anorexic being bomb-
photographed into DNA. what if the bikini was a wind that blew by us and all of us thought

28. b

of flesh and freedom? there's nothing left but to father many girls in my Lear fashion. i have no
kingdom, and so, they will thrive. there was once a snow-cone stand in my Alabama hometown.
when i drove through i saw a hammock hanging in my dead grandpa's lean-to. no wampum.
a steady stream of ice-blue seahorses from the grate on the floor harvest dust motes and traverse the
house and its littered museum. i opened the pobox and an arm reached through from the other side
its fingers trying to grab my shirt my mail dropping to the floor. out of the burning house the ashes
of our words floating across our lips making us say them again as frames.
chicken bones when we came home were arranged inexplicably in the name of our murderer.
can't afford to cut grass lion's heads of daffodils bring bees & snakes to us from neighbors' yards.
the economists' grids incinerating under flames of billowing magma; we set forth from the core.

Notes

Marcel Duchamp was a famous Dadaist, amazing chess player, artist, scultptor, Cubist,
writer, and surrealist. King Lear was a Shakesperean character based upon the Celtic
king, Leir, and, in Shakespeare's play, he is depicted as going mad and squandering his
kingdom. Lanett, Alabama is the small Alabama town I grew up in until I was around
11—the snowcone stand referenced in this section is still there upon my last visit in 2016.
Chicken bones, usually nine of then, can be used to divine the future.

29.

last night saw a guy drive a nail into wooden stake with one shot from pistol. great thought.
i've not seen starlight for several days. face is weighed down with locusts. i stare into loam.
it's intense when you realize that Pablo Picasso was one of the greatest physicists of our times.
a door is held open by a book; better consider reading it before closing it. just some wisdom.
dying is running fast with a coiled phone cord; it rips out of receiver; you say "Hello?" curtains.
you are the greatest flood i have ever had. i think about a world called Ocean. i am Earthling.
all of my bones are seahorses. no one knows my outsides are stormclouds. i have a snout-horn.
i really really want to fuck the Spanish girls like my wife really wants to fuck the Spanish guys.
i can't pull triggers. any of them. i can cock but not fire. it's cutting my balls off. i shoot pool.
lizards & cockroaches are crawling everywhere like a brain and my brain writes electric lizards.

Notes

Pablo Picasso was a famous multi-genre Cubist artist of the 20th century.

30.

i learned color from oceans of others; planets other than those others; i learned hue was quantum.
curve, not line, when we line we curve against possible geometry in DNA. writhing, then, please.
tweezers pluck my eyes and scissors cut the tendrils of my age; i'd still want to steal their visions.
aphelion, apogee, ascending node, aspect, celestial equator, conjunction, occultation. navigation.
i poke armadillo carcass with end of bamboo pole know martyr's body was poked same fashion.
moon-god dwells in Kuzina, weather-god dwells in Kummiya, in green Babylon dwells Marduk.
being of peasant stock, my Cubist vision slowly progressed until i learned how to make those lines
occupy their 3-d space geological cathedral—ice herald—glacier miners—pioneers in tow—
earth's face shaped by crystal armies engulfed in emptiness but not a Buddhist—this really bothers
me—junipers burning. this i slake pulling teeth with hatchets, bulldozers, my deputees.

Notes

Aphelion is the point of orbit of a planet when it is the furthest from the sun. Apogee is
the point in the orbit of the moon or a satellite at which it is furthest from the earth—it
also means climax or ultimate point. Kuzina is the realm of the Sumerian Moon God.
Kummiya was the city of the weather-god, Teshub, in Hittite mythos.

31.

i have been hammered like a precious metal used for battle. my crude utilitarian shapes.
i have drank much marnuwan. i am bleeding verger. the battle was supposed to be mock. i died.
Jesse James was a Virgo. that explains a lot. Yeats was a Gemini like me. that explains a lot.
when i was young i would put Elmer's glue all over my hands just to peel it off. now sunburns.
orthostats of monstrous genii carved into stone as i place my kilt strategically over my hard-on.
honeybee colonies do not cotton to a migrant lifestyle. they are communists. nectar-suckers.
as a child i had a weiner-dog named Moondog. this came from watching Star Wars. ran away.
shrimps' molts tied to lunar cycles. the new moon gives them dark place, graver water, to thrive.
the science of mold and how to feed a goat to get a certain fatty consistency to curd your life.
apple cider vinegar plus nutrient rich enzymes. i can gain soft, radiant skin. or i could age sour.

Notes

Marnuwan is an ancient ritual beer recipe from Hittite society. Jesse James was a famous outlaw and political guerilla from Missouri in post-Civil War American times. William Butler Yeats was a famous Irish poet associated with the Golden Dawn. Orthostrats are upright stones or slabs forming part of a structure or set in the ground. Genii are magical and supernatural beings found in Arab and Islamic folklore. Moondog was a dachshund, my first pet ever. Stars Wars is a cult-classic movie about a conflict between rebel and imperial forces.

32.

i was spurned there which is more street-cred than burned and then i sojourned with my gats.
i have had the beartrap snapped on me so many times that i have become a mouse or wolfen.
moon like a diseased grapefruit and you snoring by the hot spring naked—bad omens, portents.
during most days, a crow on the barbed wire fencepost is not an omen of anything, not usually.
the saddest lives were never mine nor were the happiest ones but i enjoyed my cautious dives.
a few times in my life were air-mattress times or Ramen noodle times or both. those were good.
the plastic pool outside full of water got struck by lightning and die-cast toys became diamonds.
cans of coconut milk and curry—sea salt—herb garden sunspot-scorched—we clean the last fish.
sleep Dino, sleep. words are always endangered like a tall brontosaurus who is bulimic. hovers.
an asteroid, like a pear, falls into a grove where we are starving; the buzz of it is pornographic.

Notes

Gat is slang for a gangster gun. Ramen Noodles, in the sense that I am referencing them, are cheap rip-offs of good Ramen cuisine found in every grocery store for a dollar or so, and they sustained many poor college students with their carb and sodium rich version of sustenance. "Dino" is a reference to dogs and dinosaurs courtesy of the cartoon, The Flintstones.

33.

with my mouth full of feathers i realize i can't write myths for farmers. i need shovel-spades.
zippered portraits floodtide—western ballad with your shingles—i lost my driver's lozenge.
i like ranting. i like manta rays. manta-esque. sting rays. things that glide. great angels flawed.
a caterpillar creature told me i had a pharmacy to suck up to. i cut that worm in a million pills.
that time of day when the fray is initially over—when you pause, are okay with it. it: its teeth.
i load prayers into slingshots, strapolate them propulsed through soft prey—tearing canvases.
i want orange eyes like the embers of your first campfire when you thought nothing but flame.
the words like corkscrews stuck into the corners of my mouth and i was heavy metal poisoning.
why make me the wolf only to let me age the marmet? amphibious. no trekker of snow deserts.
when i call you raucous you break the lyre and when i call you a liar you rake the haggard yard.

Notes

The caterpillar creature and pharmacy references are connected to drug innuendos in
Lewis Carroll's Alice's Adventures in Wonerland. Heavy metal poisoning occurs as a result
of industrial exposure, air or water pollution, foods, medicines, improperly coated food
containers, or the ingestion of lead-based paints.

34.

when the greatest bastards of my generation howled, it only rattled cubicles. quad-life crisis.
the junky soul traverses the infinite until there is nothing left to gorge upon. Mummu. your kiss.
i threw a ramekin and broke the kitchen window angry at you. a ridiculous moment in my life.
i faithed my way into a job i lost faith in but then i found new phoenix volcanoes and said light.
i used camou to see Grunewald's Crucifixion knowing Pollock just wanted to paint crucifixions.
you fauvist of Moreland, Georgia forests. you want good armchair. comfortable color. no faux.
massive, unfathomable drift, your fabric about all there is, my short spin here of the sphere. off.
my office, crow's nest. blackbird alights on black streetlamp. students ride elevators to gnosis.
the key to this: what i play while i write and then fuse and hope for miracle or accident. hoping.
rapid turnover printmaker collusion cornucopia bored as hells that are macro/micro and insular.

Notes

The first line of this poem is a reference to Allen Ginsberg's poem "Howl". Mummu is an ancient Sumerian deity and also means, basically, the unformed mass or chaos of the universe. Grunewald's painting, The Crucifixion, is a particularly brutal depiction of Christ on the cross, and he appears to be covered in skin lesions, most likely caused by ergotism, which was treated by the monks who requisitioned the painting. I coupled this reference with a nod to Jackson Pollock, the Abstract Expressionist painter, who struggled with religion in his own life. Fauvism was an early 20th century movement of painters who favored the use of colors for different purposes than their Impressionistic brothers. Moreland, Georgia is where this book began, and it is the setting for most of the small town and rural background of this text. If I am referring to a backyard, a back porch, a magnolia tree, etc., it was in Moreland.

35.

when a poor rib rubs against a rich ear with cancer the marrow is the same montage of roadkill.
i memorize tags on cars for fun they record my one tag for i am Tiamat and could chaos them.
monks shed tropes to traverse thoughts; makes robes necessary—phoenix clothes in monastaries.
nothing ever happens nothing ever happened to you life just passes right-wise through you.
i have one foot it is called a mind and it is webbed and there is nothing left to swim in tonight.
underground in your eyelids underground in your desks underground when you adjust a bra.
illuminating scene with a novelty; Christmas toy its lights changing like blurred traffic beacons.
i never liked lilacs. i never awaited spring. i am no war-monger; my life was made of firewood.
the worst ghosts linger about water. drowning seaweed ghosts. i carry them with me on trains.
counterfitting: a tough racket when baskets of bills mean less than piles of bones under bracken.

Notes

Tiamat is the Sumerian goddess of the ocean. The line here, beginning with "nothing", is
a bastardized and stolen lyric from the Deerhunter song, "Nothing Ever Happened".

36.

when the marble ran out, they used flowers to make the deathmasks, and those rotted aloof.
i love to smoke weed only four times a year. in ritual. its clusters in my lungs and addled stars.
i was speck of ash on phoenix wing and it rose so high; then i fell slowly, saw such wild worlds.
i notoriously break wristwatches. once i thought this was significant. i know now it's timing.
quantum field, you fuckers. galaxies spraying us with particles, and i spray back in spry ways.
i only cry once a year. i hold a pen-knife. a mollusk somewhere puffs about in beautiful sand.
what great gods keep dropping chum into this ocean of words making me shark-mad with blood.
i love Anubis friends but not really Osiris friends but at parties we all drink awesome hemlock.
my fingers have been in the warmest places and inside of the wives of the worlds. primordial.
Reality TV gladiators and producer empires give us bread and theatre. drone-suckers, all of us.

Notes

Deathmasks are masks of a person's face, afther he or she has died, made from a mould
and cast. Anubis was the jackal-headed Egyptian god of the afterlife. Osiris was the
Egyptian god of transformation and resurrection. Hemlock is a poisonous flowering
herb—it was used in ancient Greece to kill prisoners or condemned individuals—the
most famous of these being Socrates. Reality TV is a genre of programing that I wish
would disappear forever.

37.

there is a catch to everything i say. i once flew rockets. now i sit amongst you. paying homage.
i am mostly goat. the rest of me is an ox-octopus. i am kept in caves. i make you pay to see me.
i like cuticles. i'm one. a semicircular bloody thing. sty on your friend's eye. don't look too long.
i cry too much. i cried. i think i am a horror. i collect tears for vitamin waters. give you my best.
i ran across the ice until it was skating towards the traintrack and knowing a collision was birth.
burnt comic books. flooded ones. mildewing. Secret Wars we bought at the SPECTRUM. whorls.
took drug that made me covered in scales for 7 hours. roughly. i was a fish losing many friends.
eggs. potential. parmesan. careful salt. paprika. i love the sizzle when i crack and drop it. yolks.
picking up crab-apples freckled with what i would learn was parasites; i also had freckles of rot.
i drink like Modigliani. i sketch like Modigliani. i drug like Modigliani. elliptical like Modigliani.

Notes

An ox-octopus is just a reference to any sort of strange chimera carnival creature people
would possibly pay to see. Marvel Comics' Secret Wars, the original series, was published
between 1984-1985—I would ride my bike to the SPECTRUM, a convenience store
chain which sold comic books, once a month, to get the new serial. The drug which
made me itch was a bottle of Robotussin cold medicine—in college, for a cheap thrill, we
would steal these at Wal-Mart and drink them down—this was called "Robo-ing". Crab-
apples, as we called them when I was a kid, are bitter, sour apples which are full of malic
acid—we would eat them with salt. Amedeo Modigliani was a painter and a sculptor,
known for his work at the end of the 19th century and beginning of the20th century, and
for his elongated portraits of his subjects.

38.

this line is deadpan: _____.
the Foxhead bar is where we drank at Iowa. bet they don't drink there no more. try Mike's Tap.
in my mind animal shapes are sometimes genital shapes which are animal shapes and morphing.
my thoughts are webbed. the wolf spider in my study i killed. his leathery body. he has no webs.
i found new facts today affirming my beliefs in new physics and old gods. as it is below/above.
what is a pod? a polliwog? a cephalopod? a nod of besot Magog? ancient seeds, secrets, wombs.
i am not ointment for any abrasion nor salve—they take me and stab me into maple trees for sap.
i had it all sitting on top of the world, but i threw it away just to prove i could. my emo guitars.
spasms of time capsules and broken bones shred pork muscles—bricks. familiar bricks. smells.
like ants that ride other ants to fend off flying parasites we carry our leaves back to the caves.

Notes

The Foxhead is a bar in Iowa City, home of the Iowa Writers Workshop, which I attended
from 1996-1998—this bar, in my work, has come to represent a pretentious place to
hang out versus Mike's Tap, a now defunct Iowa City dive, where I preferred to drink. I
do still highly recommend the Deadwood, if, indeed, it still exists in Iowa City. Magog
was a son of Japheth, from Biblical history, who supposedly fathered what would become
the Nordic tribes. The line beginning "I had it all…" is from Taking Back Sunday's song,
"Where My Mouth Is".

39.

as a young man, i followed father's wishes and became a lawyer. lo and behold i lech the lore.
i want to work in a traincar that sells toy trains by a traintrack and have my studio engineered.
no butterfly ever kissed the broken windshield but purple crowshit laced it with abstract paint.
you run through like a prairie dog with foam slathering your jowls and nothing here loves you.
painting is the "transcription of the adventures of the optic nerve". thank you, Bonnard, i see.
a student told me he ate octopus, whole octopus, in Georgia. i eat students. funny sea creatures.
hollow of pillow cradles the infected ear with reverb from dad's Stratocaster in the back hovel.
you can no longer blame all of these broken dishes on poltergeist activity. please ghost the ghost.
alas, Atlas, you dropped the world on your toe and it swoll-up into another world. what now?
you wave like you should be on a float in a parade your wave a weathervane free from winds.

Notes

Pierre Bonnard described painting as the "transcription of the adventures of the optic nerve". The Fender Stratocaster electric guiar is referenced several times in this long series of poems. Atlas was a Titan of Greek mythology who led an army of Titans against Zeus—for this, he was punished to hold the heavens up upon his back for eternity.

40.

when i hang my skin up on the hook every night, it hovers over me. i try to hide in others' hurts.
you woke up with a mountain on your face. a pressure. now you hold a volcano in your hand.
in December, i hung my October costumes about the palisade to make ghosts look for gods.
i skin selves of my self all the time. it makes good omens for kids. live woodwise. constellate.
i rehab. i re-again. your quilts are amazing. i shred them. i need to be strong as guitar strings.
no one sleeps here anymore. i looked at porn to try. no one sleeps here anymore. ravens galore.
wrench and clench me into a plier-man a man torn; be teeth a socket set of cannibal teeth i love.
henchmen guitar punk goliaths want to kill youths because of the slings and bright lights loudly.
860 letters to Theo about alchemy. i walked Arles; felt vacant. no francs. no butterfly pigment.
Spanish moss makes all of us warm because it sparks the bug skeletons into all-night cinders.

Notes

There is a David and Goliath references here in terms of "slings". My text references
the painter Vincent Van Gogh's letters to his brother, Theo, and suggests that they
were alchemical in nature. Arles is where Van Gogh was said to have done some of his
best paintings and also where he was hospitalized for a time due to his mental health. I
mention Spanish Moss here because, when I lived in Savannah, Georgia, I was told not to
handle it because it was full of skin mites—in this section, I imagine the bugs burning in
the moss used for kindling.

41.

you write and the fresco explodes across my mind and i see one blossom in it and meld plaster.
where i live there are no rivers. moon cruel in our bones. thirst is a moon. trapped around core.
the only angel you will ever meet is good peat—a place to dog and listen to seedpod futures.
my meninas, your spun worlds against my barbed worlds make incredible robes for futures.
the guitar grabbed me & broke me on the floor and my strings flew into melodic shaman-space.
you've been cornered by a beautiful angel. worst moment of your life. she extracts and thrums.
cartoon eyelids make bad cloud movies but i still watch as if a storm had a moral or i am candy.
the wars were dancers when you do the math. ceremonial life was only a way to map collateral.
i had every chance to quit private jihad but i stood against the wall and became the beds of stars.
i stood in Civil War graveyard with my step-daughter tonight and she held my hand steadfast.

Notes

A menina is a young girl. A Jihad is the term for a Muslim holy war. The Civil War graveyard I refer to in this poem is Founders Cemetery in Moreland, Georgia.

42.

i don't try to syncopate hate i try to hummingbird so fate smiles as we slip by it with doubloons.
your wayward talisman letter gave me shivers as i walked towards the pobox knowing the ache.
thoroughbred thoughts in my head and nascent memories in my loins and like an aegis i hover.
all that work for so much pain, that pain for such great work. when you think shame, shimmer.
you erased me from the holy roster, and i followed you home stabbing you with colored pencils.
Hammond Organ i feel sick Hammond Organ i am stoned Hammond Organ i am nostalgic. Z's.
frenetic brushwork and vigorous powerful thrusts caking the oil about the orchid's lips. terse.
never use the word "sorcerer" in a poem—are you serious? you conjure mothmen like C.I.A.
you have honey on your tongue. beeswax in your ears. you sway while tied. a tree in tempest.
my chariot of charades or charade of chariots—it is unclear but we cut a vainglorious swath of it.

Notes

"Pobox" is slang for p.o. box—in Moreland, we had no mailbox and were poor, thus we rented the "po" box at the Post Office in Newnan, Georgia. The Aegis is the goatskin shield of Zeus or Athena in Classical Greek mythology. The Hammond Organ has a very distinctive sound which I remember from growing up in the seventies. Mothmen is plural for the Mothman, a legendary creature of American folklore and conspiracy theory fame. The C.I.A., or Central Intelligence Agency, is said to be behind the Mothman, among other heinous things. In Homer's Odyssey, sailors stuff beesway into their ears in order to resist the songs of the Sirens who would crash them upon the rocks—this implies that these men had honeycombs on board...

43.

i chopped Eden down; made a ship and planted it in the desert. no flood myths. just business.
in football, they only wear pads so that they can do it again. otherwise, mangled bodies galore.
Woden was a one-eyed son of a bitch and his own son accidentally hit him with a hammer once.
so it comes to Li Po again. my friend David wrote:"Weary of moonlight, the moon...". drowned.
when i listen to Interpol i often think of what Paul Banks listens to with his girl. it's not Interpol.
it's all decrompression breakfast club fallout recomissioned wanna-be-neo-chic death chambers.
i never cut my hands off; you did. all stood in pools of my blood. they shivered in glee and sank.
i started printing that shit everyday like i might die the next day so i'd have it that day, y'know?
it's owls or eagles. you fly or desecrate. which do you want? battlefield goggles? crow's wings?
i have never been able to hold beauty in my hands for too long. Pegasus feathers are lessons.

Notes

Woden is the chief god of the Scandinavian Anglo-Saxon tribes, and his son is Thor. Li Po
was an 8th century Chinese poet, during the Tang Dynasty, who wrote a great deal about
wine and most likely died from it. The David I refer to in this poem is an old friend of
mine, the poet, David Callan. Paul Banks is the lead singer of the post-punk rock band
Interpol. The breakfast club I refer to here is based upon the film, The Breakfast Club.

44.

i am drunk and stunned sitting here writing. i hope you are engorged in living great lives.
shuck your shell and hand it to me and i will sell it for better skin to a snake-venom vendor.
the Schwinger representation is useful for making manifest the particle aspect of a propagator.
my hands are on fire but i can't put them out my hands are on fire but i can't put them out. songs
every creature that i ever met should have drank with me or did or i drank their swill laughing.
i decided to put empty fortune cookies in everyone's pockets today and i hope i cause carwrecks.
Gauguin killed his nuns with brown rumps. i kill mine with fat beats. you know my henchmen?
i am the greatest expert in dehydration having tried it upon myself a lifetime while spilling ink.
one of my favorite bands says "spare me the suspense." i would rather be spared this worn flesh.
pawnshacks are hearts on terrible roads. we need mechanics and English majors. we need dorks.

Notes

"Snake-venom vendor" refers to "snake oil" vendors of the American old West who would
sell "linements" which promised to be cure-alls for ailments but were bogus medicines in
reality. Schwinger Representation consists "of a finite or compact simple Lie group is set
up as a multiplicity-free direct sum of all the unitary irreducible representations of the
group." Gauguin was a painter, during the time of the aforementioned Van Gogh, who
was a very influential artist of the Symbolist movement and who was known widely for
his paintings regarding the subject of Tahiti. The quote, "spare me the suspense", is a lyric
stolen from the band Interpol's song "Mammoth".

45.

i never see the sunrise. i go from bed to office. early. a dusk always twilight world i teach in.
animated crowd punctuates background like windchimes muffled by monstrous transactions.
i was healed in secret places, squeamish places, places of ill repute. i was restored in ill filth.
at the punk show i got to play a solo and it was wonderful and i could not fuck it up it rocked.
i have a beartrap hand. i can never write without damage. i catch things i shouldn't. can't piss.
preternatural hummingbird terrified me—that probiscus and that outboard motor buzzing.
the summer at Craig's when the fleas infested the hardwood floors a terrible scratching plague.
i heard something in the guitar reached in and found a card seven spades and let it fall back.
your voice like something stuck in resin scatters down the stairs painting them amber, ochre.
awe-sapped, slouched back far into the couch, relinquished, a boiled peanut husk from a can.

Notes

At a punk show, where the many incarnations of bands, which many of my students were in, were playing, I was allowed onstage, in Peachtree City, Georgia, to wail away on the guitar. The probiscus of assorted bugs has become a vampire symbol in Western culture. "The summer at Craig's" references when I stayed with Craig Varian across the street from West Georgia College and we were eaten alive by fleas. The Seven of Spades card represents a persona which is seeking higher truths but can only achieve them through ultimate faith.

46.

hard knuckle of pine-knot cut from the deadfall for an inkblot and then it petrifies slow-like.
if you turned over the Tarot card to find your own visage which card would you look out from?
the fabric truck crashed and the thousands of balls of twine unraveled across the traffic. omens.
calligraphy of ivy grows about the shower window as mold and mildew crust black clouds.
gentle voice through the phone and i am in jail waiting for powdered eggs. Hope out tomorrow.
took the crowbar thrashed through the dishes section of the mega-mart and no one called cops.
they have the greatest cubicles in heaven that you will ever see. i have this on expert authority.
writing about Surrealist painting only exists as a form of love said de facto Andre Breton to me.
the vorticism created in self-mythos of the ley lines which must have pulled us here. spiders.
always hoping for less dross, for ways to make trapdoors under everything. fall to foam worlds.

Notes

Tarot cards have been referenced before in this text and in the notes. The paintings of
the Surrealists focused upon imagery involved with dreamscapes and the interpretation
of dreamscapes and what Salvador Dai called the paranoic critical method. Andre Breton
was, amongst other things, a writer and painter, and he is credited with writing the first
Surrealistic Manifesto in 1924.

47.

this arbor of books and pines while i fantasize of desert—it's wiped clean face awaiting forests.
i have not seen my own breath in the air for so long. i miss my shadow like that. star departs.
i have the violence of quickly pulled tinfoil; its flesh ready to mold to every shape silverscaped.
i was told that she liked collecting buttons. like a compulsion. does she want to open or close us?
aphid and centipede invade at times. this old home does not leak water it births vermin. fine.
trapped inside the crashlanding locust, and she is only about eating the harvest. please birth me.
what did my father want? what did my mother want? his joints in the shed. her hysterics. help.
i am convinced that i have pinworms. i've had them before. did not know. my ass itched badly.
i often think about the end of guitar strings. we'll have to go back to guts of cats. messier bizness.
the most awful thing i ever heard filled me with awe. i was in a time machine. a lynched squaw.

Notes

I got pinworms as a child from eating mudpies I made in a Holly Hobby oven—
pinworms are an intestinal parasite that make your ass itch because the females lay their
eggs around the anus. Strings for acoustic instruments were often made from something
called "catgut", but, in actuality, catguts were not used—most instruments were strung
from fibers from the guts of goats and other animals. A squaw is an English equivalent
word for the Algonquian word meaning "woman".

48.

i can place things here that would alienate you. i could welcome you. i could kill you and twist.
you can skin an animal but not a mountain. actually, you can sin a mount. it's a plastic echo.
to make the rainbow. your strap down across your shoulder. the sun coaxing your skin-tones.
punching a clock is a knuckle-fest you tech-school mavens and now steal the fermented dials.
in spines of books are the dogs never wounded or never heard whining. cloak thyself in spines.
you set up towers. you set up days. you excurse into cruises. you carefully season my corpse.
i cut my hand off and gave it to a man with thousands of hands and cast out my ridden cash.
rivulets of crash and rivulets of brash wet toes as they flow towards the vast welkin terrains.
figurehead wild beast of especially. and usually, especially was denied all of us normal drums.
wind across the belly and am ashamed as fish die before me in the seagreen pastures of offices.

Notes

The word, "welkin", is one of my favorites—a very neglected word—it means "the sky" or heaven—but mainly, I think, the upper heavens.

49.

i wander my own house like i would wander any wilderness. boys forget. men remember this. have no
fangs, only quicksilver—i draw a bead on them snakes and shoot their unholy eyes out.
no one ever played with their heart. their heart played with them. in between were quiet ninjas.
how many mailboxes have you left that you find out later are flying airbuses? no returns hereto.
none of my rural murals completed after my stowaway stint from Netherlands. i submarined.
black panes in the pain of winter. cold touch toe or nipple or word. need for salty smoked fish.
i rode high as gods holding the antlers of the angel and i was tossed when she left us all to molt.
hemp spiderweb and the talcum and the burned hands and the resin and the tarp and red clay.
i never paid the bills; they flanked me one night in the forest by the collapsed bridge. i begged.
onions caramelize slowly as my daughter spins circles on the hardwood floors and garlic sizzles.

Notes

Quicksilver is a reference to liquid metal, or mercury, or something that is faster than a
snake's strike. The "Netherlands" reference does not actually refer to that region on the
planet Earth—in my context, it means the voids or the nothing lands—an abyss that is
unfortunately inhabitable.

50.

there are singing bones under us at all times and sometimes you say words: singing bones.
your bass-lines pound me into playing bass so that i hump better thromboid erogenous zones.
i had cellular currency. brain or muscle. wasted DNA. i breathe. collateral damage. worship, yo.
i alley down; shadows chase and not the other way around. i climb on the posts and snuff cities.
i called everyone drunk with my machine guns, and no one was wounded but me. i dismount.
bewilderingly rapid turnover to usurp or stratify or endeavor to cube or stencil what one can.
this amazing world relents my butterfly. my butterfly crashes across battlefield helmet noses.
i see it look for problems—things to get spores from; you are butterfly king but you look around
and drop your cellphone while the girl named Mariposa texts that you are dead. dross totem.
walking in the house you spotted a large locust & thumbed it. needed me to be bigger, biggest.

Notes

Mariposa is the Spanish word for butterfly.

51.

painting. photography. printmaking. within same frame. transfer-drawn. obscura. multifarious.
i was thinking cartoon trees, mainly spruce, and then walked outside to see cartoon ants on them.
Janus, i love your faces. do they see me more than i see you, or myself? do you ever look away?
my spine a blind man's cane. my desires the seeing-eye dog. the soul on 1000 unknown streets.
who adjusts my wavelength allowing me to be here writing this now & astral whenever & often?
i am a slave just like you once were. i hold the remote remotely. you hold a tear forever. morons.
i used to tear my jeans on soft grass because i crash-ripped so hard. they'd patch it with jeans.
whose bed would you sleep in? what great man or woman? whose redbugs would you share?
hendecasyllabic rispetto. ottava rima. epic. strambotto. dactylic hexameter is my favorite. Iliad.
i just came back from burning the forests of my masks. i was hospitalized briefly. given alms.

Notes

Janus is the two-headed Roman god who looks to the present and the past
simultaneously—he is the god of beginnings and endings. Redbugs are what we call the
parasites, chiggers, and I am mixing this idea with bedbugs, who are even tougher to get
rid of. "hendecasyllabic rispetto--dactylic hexameter"—this list refers to different poetic
metrics, and is a nod to the epic poem by Homer, The Iliad, and a nod to the fact that I
am trying to write an epic myself.

52.

all ideas fell like confetti and then nailed down the pinewood floors under me with screams.
stepdaughter calls the carpenter bee lame because he can't bumble into the hole. cruel nature.
a bridge is not always a harp or an altar—sometimes it is a gamble of taut decisions with vines.
the Spanish Armada finishing its conquests through our tongues all the way to Canada. gringos.
yellow shotgun shell in muckpuddle with petals of lottery tickets. dog trips on acid as he walks.
panting like a televangelist at a porn convention. a slack-jowled yokel. need to break my leash.
bluetick hound buckshot and bleeding. hyena in a landfill. territorial intervals. beartrap nights.
i have a dream catcher. it's a slingshot. fires them off the minute they are done. eyelids twitchin'.
lost housekey is a gendarme mindfuck. when you lose a key, you find out who your family is.
i think i should check you for ticks. you are rabid at best in your pantsuit. wildflower, you reek.

Notes

Carpenter bees are one of 500 species of bees who like to bore holes into your back porch during spring and summer months—I wrote many sections of this book while sawdust fell around me from the rafters from their work. The line about the bridge not always being a harp or an altar is a reference to Hart Crane. The Spanish Armada was a fleet of 130 ships deployed during an undeclared war. A slack-jawed yokel is someone in awe with their mouth hanging open. A bluetick hound is a dog with hanging jowls mainly used to hunt raccoons. A Dream-catcher is an object co-opted form the Ojibwa tribe which has become a stereotypical symbol of Native Americans and is generally taken out of context. The gendarme, in my context, is both meanings of the word—a police force and a rock formation to be overcome.

53.

ode to immrama. i tore off your sails like ripping pages. sing Sirens and melt the wax and wreck.
Esemplastic. Gonadotrophin. Borborgysms. Vermicular. Jactation. Inimical. Stochastic. Aleatory.
the cell phone towers burn so bright tonight. i parachute through your multi-media. your virtual.
scarecrow smile. shipwreck torso. graveyard teeth. some thought you full of feathers. not me.
if i must i'll be the tongue of the swaggering forward beast with its knees and fangs making war.
i want Chuck Close to paint the freckles on my arm using elixirs of melted freckles and pigment.
impossible to love. a plum blossom in a wolf's mouth. conundrum in an elevator. or a Viking
in an office building swinging axes. i find it hard to swallow poisonous jellyfish all day and call
it all bureaucracy and appendages stinging me with spreadsheets and spiked deadlines. grimace.
a billion guitars to be played marching towards a billion commoners and they clash. a good war.

Notes

The Immrama is a collection of seafaring tales from ancient Ireland which chronicles
questors trying to find The Otherworld. Sirens are vixens who sing sailors to their deaths
upon rocks. "Esemplastic—Aleatory"—refers to the endocrine system of your body.
Chuck Close is known as an amazing photorealist modern/postmodern painter.

54.

i see myself now. i put down the knife, the bottle, the pen. i levitate while coffin-siting. i see now.
driving barefoot to liquor store. spend last $5. drank in a church parking lot. Merle Haggardly.
suck down pharms for hard-ons. gyrate & spill give voice to swill. the falcon lost its falcon gene.
wish i could tie myself to a javelin and get thrown your way stabbing into truth of earth. shunk.
strings break. instrument reclaims the man who plays her. he comes home with slinky bronzen.
mosquitoes are always shaving my beard. people drag Christmas trees up stairs losing needles.
my thumb meets smiter as i get nailed down. it hurt. i was always dumb as a bag of hammers.
winged things navigate massacres. swift lithe uzi teeth. in heaven blood up to your ankles. awe.
you only see history as ruins. poems have sundrenched eyelids. you blind to both? stones talk.
human speech once swaddled in root of oak now on streets in asphalt cracks wry seepage song.

Notes

Merle Haggard is an amazing country music singer/songwriter poet whose name I
turned into an adverb. "The falcon lost its falcon gene" is a reference to the Yeats' poem,
"The Second Coming." The Uzi was designed by Uziel Gal and is a submachine gun—
incidentally, "Uzziel" is an angel, mentioned in Enochian text, whose name means
"Strength of God".

55.

how else would i learn to love a child but to navigate my addict wife. i do the best that i can.
turkey vultures do their ballet in the front yard of a guy i do not know. i want to know him now.
to disappear costs so much money. to be invisible is easy. always buy notes you never write.
at all costs one must do things at all costs. if one has no bankroll, then he must handjob forever.
the universe has before & after pics. we download them on phones. we lick stars. press send.
do you think that it was all out to get me or was i all out to get it? was it pearls and blossoms?
whiskey cleans nothing. paint-thinner. moonshine. one cleans more things by not speaking ill of.
tried to catcha ghost, some tiny assemblage of iron filings responded. it was stop-motion anime.
Cookie 3 5 8 10 26 27: "You will win favors when you expand your social circle." We want salvos.
a phrase that makes a sound in your mouth: papaya rum caramel sauce. a phrase of diabetes #2.

Notes

Line nine is from a fortune cookie—play the lottery numbers if you please. Diabetes Type
2 is conquering America.

56.

you saw a lightning bug once. you were a child. now you moth towards convenience stores.
what could have been meets the thing it was supposed to be and they drink coffee laughing.
pinball machines rust while terrorists conspire. it's all magnificent somehow. backpack nukes.
i made a pizza once. i made two. a Chicago and a New York. then i made you choose a shore.
humility is a crust on the cusp of a crest of those whose lineage could evolve towards suns.
she sweeps the floors all day after the haircuts her mind full of histories and sweet forgets.
Mavis at the Waffle House at exit 41 Highway 89 south. Mavis with few teeth and less advice.
buckshot stop signs. rebel flags. cowhide attire. Orion chasing the bear near austere moonsickle.
bushwacked world of locust mutilations. the veins in his hands becoming guitar strings. cables.
putting the monster of ten-thousand universes into the closet & young daughter never opened it.

Notes

The Waffle House on Highway 85 South, at the Moreland, Georgia exit, which is close
to where I lived when I started this book, was presided over by Mavis—a belligerent, but
wholly wonderful, waitress. If you drive around the country, particularly in the South,
you will see signs with buckshot holes in them. Orion is the hunter who chases Ursa
Major and the Great Pyramids align with his belt.

57.

my satyr hands my satyr hooves my satyr wallet my satyr lawyer my satyr love affairs. tumbles.
counting the same ceiling fan blade until cancer comes home to my bones and then alight i do.
any true altercation only happens when tectonic plates smash. what? a true particle could eat all.
he notched the gun so many times that it had no stock. a trigger. a barrel. useless fuselage. lesson.
one dollar Dollar-General hourglass egg-timer on desk and this was once the way to stall the sun.
problem with killing sacrificial beasts: the ones we are always killing are totem avatars. damned.
a factory of lamps a wasp nest in the corner of the hangar and one flies into a machine honorably.
the greatest place ever known was the place that something ate so when i learned to eat i had to.
a man tried to kill me once but his icepick struck gold and a blood sausage was his last supper.
kayaked through you kayaked to you kayaked in you kayaked with you. i sacrificed with you.

Notes

Satyrs, in the Greek sense, have horse or donkey ears and horse or donkey tails. Tectonic
Plate Theory was once controversial and states that the outer crusts of the Earth float
around upon lakes of magma. The Dollar General is a discount store with thousands of
locations in the United States. There is a loose reference to Trotsky with the icepick in line
nine.

58.

wings come with a lack of responsibility. broken backs come with a lot of cops. fabrications. guts.
i will push. through you. you sent data to the cloud. it hit your droid. slowly responding debris.
all of my friends are mutts. i too am a miscreant of genes and circumstance. let's fingerpaint.
my nose is always cold like a dog's nose. that means i am healthy. either a wolf or a fast friend.
chariot. heth. cancer. khepera, Apollo. crab, turtle, sphinx, lotus. on the cusp. cut glass. Sunkist.
yowling you bring the morels and dried olives. the electricity is out. we begin thinking of fuel.
using this seashell to scoop coffee-grounds. i notice you replace it with a plastic spoon. why i cry?
the things you straightline should be crooked. trainwrecks and newborns. your fears and starch.
the best math of the universe created dumbass us. frustrating crumbs on top of quantum detritus.
the insignificant bang is as good as the big one. a moose wanders out of a forest into it. settling.

Notes

Chariot, hesth, cancer, khepera, etc. and Sunkist—line five of this poem references many
things regrding the Zodiac and also the soda-pop "Sunkist".

59.

strength. teth. leo. bastet, sekhmet. lion. sunflower. lava cools and we make wedding rings. uff.
666. a fiddle and fire. Iphone and bar codes. download more hits & aps. sit complacent in the Guf.
i am on the threshold and want to kiss someone before falling over the edge. pretty hyacinths.
navigate bricabrac. broken beer bottle wine cooler. Etruscan statue pot with weeds growing in it.
locusts fly around me as i walk through the tall grass, and they are training for the next plague.
books flying aross acres towards reconciliation in arabesque, but the confederacy is suffocating.
pungent burlesque moribund succubus signature of derelict wanton orphan goddess breaks us.
new cats on the porch eating all of our W.I.C. voucher tuna. this is a turning point i think tonight.
noodlers come to steal guitars. we educate them and kill them. give them neckslash diplomas.
a lifelong row for us all. we hate it hanging over us. it drips like a dog's jowls. keep paddling.

Notes

Teth, leo, bastet, Sekhmet, etc.—this list is derived from the Egyptian Zodiac. 666 is
a reference to the Roman emperor, Nero. The Guf is the Treasury of Souls in Jewish
mysticism. The Etruscan pottery I am referring to in this poem is of the bucchero ilk.
W.I.C. Vouchers were once given to families who needed government assistance for
food because of low income households—before that, they were food stamps—now it's
all on a card. Noodlers are guitar players who incessantly solo or "jam" to the point of
masturbatory pointlessness.

60.

TV silver light on my arm as i fillet wild boar. who will i feed this meat to in the ether? Motel 6.
ailment. absinthe. antidote. bards. the withdrawals of great white expanses. pure killing random.
if a woman is a navigable tower then waves crash on her shore. she makes you into ships, pilots.
we were looking for marijuana whether we realized it or not. the first time we smelt it. goodness.
you wear your circuitry like a beard. cellphones for ears. they won't even call them phones soon.
i am Shao-Lin master. i am pumpkin seed. i am fairy-dust. i am carburetor. i am wounded bear.
i am distant buoy. i am Nick's quadricept. i am a dice-roll. i am candor. i am chicken feathers.
i am Swedish. I am paperback. I am lamb tandoori. i am nipples of Nick McRae. am fine oh mine.
quills and marks. hunts and smokehouses. complain again and ostracized. can't argue balances.
comorants, geyser spurts, thicket, hammer and viscera. i gnaw the All's bones. it's required.

Notes

Motel 6 is a chain of inns which provides cheap rooms and, in my experience, is generally
associated with shady people and events. The Shao-Lin monks are mysterious Buddhist
martial artists. Nick McRae was an old colleague of mine at The University of West
Georgia, an amazing poet, and a man of God.

61.

St. Oran was drowned in me. he made me dig thousands of wells. fished for mermaids. none.
Banning Mill, in Whitesburg, Georgia, is where i met many ghosts and minotaurs with Sarah.
we have been making ears in my shed. they look like pig parts. they hear every knife in radius.
the earth screams all day at me and i spill my guts to it and end up being fields of wings. amen.
we will ride tortoise's towards old black men at huddle houses and they will tell us of bleedings
Cain wears the best cologne as he tills cubicles. those wall street gardens with his blood mascara.
sleeping inside pianos is ok. fungus grew under my watchband. i loved that watch. mushrooms.
flying fish crashing into a windmill. rain-splattered windshield. your speech is the effervessence.
swill all down with a bitter pill of poem. tears of gasoline. stripping flesh from the weaklings.
got the trident and the net and the begot beget. to be debonair apercu with mammoth tentacles.

Notes

St. Oran threw his body into the foundation of a temple in order to make it stand
and then rose from the dead three days later. Banning Mill is a very haunted place in
Whitesburg, Georgia where I once hung out with Sarah Strong Wilson and is now a
zip-line attraction for tourists. Cain killed his brother for putting his livestock on his
farmland. Flying fish are mentioned in this note because they may soon be extinct, but
many are still found in the Caribean.

62.

broken Icarus brother friend who i killed with shovel and laid in shallow grave i must commend.
it was like Motown, a music you can't ignore. the Taladega worlds crash into petrified forests.
i joined the snake church. i learned diamondback. i heart-rattle. i reach my arms to you forked.
i put on myth special scar overhauls. love sprouting tiger lilies, snapdragons. red tape auspice.
another barb, bend, wall, turn. avians picking roadkill. intermesh bracelet of corporal and oracle.
crumbling mortar pockmarkedwall. battlementimplements. chainlinkchakra. meat & metalpulse.
i wonder how long i will wait to murder everyone i love in a sheer great guitar solo with gods.
i want to be a lake free of messiahs. i am not one who hopes for miracles. they bring conquerors.
one night i was beaten into submission by a MAGLIGHT. light implement. i bled from temples.
i swear by rifle over your banjo. writhe through the trifle. angry Anubis soul. swagger braggard.

Notes

Icarus is always a motif in my work, and I also associate him with Cain and other figures who were disenfranchised by their own family members and those who should have protected them. Motown is a record label which helped to integrate African-American music into the mainstream—founded by Barry Gordy—and it has been a driving force of musical and spiritual freedom and awareness for half a century now. A snake-church is a place of worship where people handle live snakes to defy Satan and prove faith while drinking Mason jars of Stychnine. A diamoindback is a type of rattlesnake. Taladega racetrack is in Alabama, and it interrupts a National Forest, and I associate it with good and bad redneck, government, and commercial behavior in our culture. A MAGLIGHT is a heavy flashlight carried by a police officer. Anubis is an Egytptian god with the head of a jackal.

63.

it rains on my heart for eternity and it is fucking awesome. you are jealous and you should be.
guitar headstock rests neck on window-pane. my knuckles are made of metal and wood. kisses.
umpfucteen bad things. shooting pool. lying to myself. morning is landing like a UFO. crime.
mailbox and lunchbox. Keats and his handkerchiefs. i saw a gaunt coyote run towards the abyss.
only starfruit grew in Eden. eve had no vagina. she had salvation between her legs. Adam ran.
oracles throw bones and we break them pulling plows. our women die in childbirth. damn holy.
i tried to strangle autumn. demons came and pissed golden-red blood everywhere. i freckled.
snapping green beans into the copper bowls while squash men waited to become casseroles.
cut the grass. slur. laugh. dogwood heaves under a hailstorm. recovers. mocks you. need oil.
quarry dive on drunken Memorial Day. tattered tags of tongues. sunscreen salt and copulations.

Notes

A UFO is an unidentified flying object of course, but in the context of this book, it
is a portal as well or an interdimensional entity of sorts. John Keats was an English
Romantic poet who died way too young—the handkerchiefs reference his condition of
consumption. The dogwood tree is common in Alabama where I grew up, and there is
a story that this tree was used by the Romans for their crucifixions because of its strong
wood—this tree was supposedly once as big as an oak, but after the crucifixion of Christ,
it was transformed, by God, into the smaller tree it is now to keep it from ever being
used for human sacrifice again. The center of the flower represents the crown of thorns,
and the colored marking on the petals represent the wounds of Christ. The red dogwood,
known as the Cherokee, is supposedly red to symbolize the blood of the messiah. Quarry-
diving is a dangerous undertaking by fools who dive from cliffs into industrial mining
quarries full of rainwater and wash-off.

64.

cookies. credit cards. cookies. credit cards. the dark ages. cookies. credit cards. the dark ages.
i have the glacier cellphone app. i will deploy upon you. my three-year-old just threw up. i'll call.
parchment is what i was wrapped in and it was also my burial shroud so libraries resurrect me.
your storm in me beginning creating dark seasons to come. damn you Donald Trump Star Trek.
wingspan in my chest cavity. a coma stroke embolism aperture. wingspan in my chest cavity.
blogs guns and gaga. i will never chop down my tree but my roots are in your evangelist mouth.
i am cannibal at flesh carnival. puff pastry roadkill. powdered sugar on my lips. turkey-legs.
the idiot comes in like a tycoon. he finds the penny on heads, and he's happy. smokes his stash.
then he unleashes his tie. relaxes. he always sleeps with his eyes open. he orders beer for all.
and he can't pay. and it's Christmas. he has to walk at least twenty miles. it's love; understand?

Notes

At the time that I wrote this section, Donald Trump was not yet President of the United States—he now currently is. Star Trek is a long-running cult-favorite TV, comic book, and movie series concerned with the conflicts involved with humans and other alien races exploring the deeps of space. For some reason, I associate the Star Trek actor, William Shatner, with Donald Trump.

65.

the maw spit vampiral exodus. i was in awe at the gore. destroyed universe. nebulae. thermals.
unlucky conquistadors and concubines unluckier. Apalachee ambush of Black Fridays. holidays.
drinking artillery punch on the isthmus. a throng of admirers sucking syrup from ancient trees.
Thor and Achilles were both crossdressers. so was Sir Edmund. i like thriftshops for dresses, LPs.
no warship wind today, my traitors. no push toward GoldWhoreAldo. just doldrums and sores.
mawspit. chawspit. bowsprit. peachpit. her eyes. in the shit. scurvy fits. token misfits. false grit.
egalitarian culprits with diamond-studded brass-knuckles. no nutrition for Cerberus in this hell.
like when he hits a pedal with his foot to make it crunchy. God's gonna play his Fender louder.
with pilgrim's plight i flee a bedroom to the shower with your bipolar ass screaming dark hexes.
sachem. wigwam. moccasin. scalping. geese flying over bloodsoaked cherry trees bloompulsing.

Notes

Sherman artillery punch was a drink supposedly concocted by Southerners in Savanna, Georgia which helped dissuade Sherman from burning down the city at the end of his march in the Civil War.   Thor and Achilles both were "cross-dressers" at one point in order to achieve a goal in their mythos. Sir Edmund Andros tried to escape prison in Massachusetts, in 1686, by dressing as a woman. GoldWhoreAldo is a word I invented to represent a place where everyone is obsessed with material gain—a capitalist paradise. Cerberus is the three-headed dog in Greek myths who guards the gates to Hades. Fender is a reference to the famous electric guitar company—the Stratocaster being one of their more preferred models. Sachem is a Native American word for boss or leader. Wigwam is a Native American word for shelter.

66.

in my sloop in the shallows. longboats slip by with hooded shankers. i see those hillbillies good.
there's no regiment here. always jerkey at the quiktrips. always crystalmeth at thanksgivings.
i feel i am always in musket range of some sharpshooter and this is not paranoid is my red tattoo.
for years i thought that the Vatican was something held the porch up. then i met that plaid skirt.
guerilla squirmish for the last of the scrambled eggs. i bastion with the bacon. stop laughing you.
if i am a sawed-off then you are a Derringer and if i am a colt then you are a Howitzer. ok? now?
we made crop circles with our Harleys. blaspheming American barley. crashing into churches.
sinister entrepot of the subconscious. Dybbuk box of subconscious. minotaur-maze of energies.
the Mohegans had made allies with our enemies. they are excellent scouts. remain cautious.
under a hissing hailstorm the golden Labrador puppies were born with tin roof rattling a racket.

Notes

Shankers is a slang word I punned based on watching prison films and documentaries—
vindictive inmates would make "shanks", sharp objects frim chicken bones or
toothbrushes, to murder each other with. A Derringer is a single-shot pistol, made
by Henry Deringer in the 19th century. A Howitzer is an artillery cannon. Harleys
are motorcycles, Harley Davidsons, made by a legendary cycle company founded in
Wisconsin in 1903. A Dybbuk Box is a haunted winebox which is usually inhabited by an
evil spirit, generally associated with the Jewish tradition of lore. Mohegans were primarily
a Native American tribe in Conneticutt—their name generally translates into "people of
the wolf". Labrador puppies are a breed of dog which my parents bred when I was a boy.

67.

enjoying reading forgeries—Necronomicon, Oera Linda, documents of Constantinople. frauds.
you thought pine needle beds romantic. made adultery there. came home covered in deerticks.
copperheads and water moccasins tattooed all over your back writhing under my hard hands.
Santa Anna was a Scottish Rite Freemason. many times was his life spared with distress sign.
every night is Samhain here. sage burning. Eye of Horus. spirits walk in and swirl in coffee.
maybe you under-estimate a pair of brass knuckles and the need to get this whiskey homebound.
there are many folk devils and moral panics here. none sufficient enough to make crackers vote.
Wand. Cup. Dagger. Coin. Wheel. Axle. Altar. Staff. Spiral. Windfall. Tempest. Artifact. Chant.
Lemurians. Atlanteans. Alabamians, you laugh. how could any of us be from a more lost land?
they categorized my blood as Appalachian. i wasn't proud of this for years. now i'm changing.

Notes

The Necronomicon is a text composed by H.P. Lovecraft, and he said its contents
came to him in a dream. The Oera Linda is an ancient text, written in Frisian, which is
supposedly a forgery or hoax. Santa Anna was known as the Mexican Napoleaon, and he
was also, supposedly, inducted into a secret society as a Scottish Rite Freemason. Samhain
is the Gaelic harvest festival beginning on October 31st. The Eye of Horus, also known as
the "wedjat", is indicative of an all-seeing eye. The references of Wand through Chant are
a mixture of Tarot and ritual images and terms. Lemurians, like Atlanteans, were the once
prosperous inhabitants of a now sunken continent.

68.

Muddy Waters John Lee Hooker Buddy Guy Howlin Wolf ride the Mississippi up to Chicago.
American ships stocked with cranberries to fight scurvy. Vodka is the Russian word for water.
the Spartans made their coinage too large and heavy for the citizens to effectively steal. good.
ablutions. four showers a day. sulphuric amalgamations. nothing can be stripped from flesh.
New York hurt my liver. Nashville hurt my heart. New Orleans hurt my soul. Atlanta, the rest.
you must even have protection against songstress snakes in the underworld. learn your spells.
i'm a man of no means by every deed and am kingfisher of the brood. hobo-cults gathering.
in my dreams i fly over Georgia landscapes with helicopter POV. is this TV residue or astral?
Palace Brothers Will Oldham Bonnie Prince Billy The Pretender The Wolf Brother. campfires.
clarion calls tonight. lady of the water's arm extends from West Point Lake holding a fiddle bow.

Notes

Muddy Waters, John Lee Hooker, Buddy Guy, and Howlin' Wolf were all legendary
bluesmen. The "a man of no means" reference pertains to Roger Miller's song "King of the
Road". A kingfisher is a peculiar bird who often lives in abandoned hornets' nests. Palace
Brothers, Bonnie Prince Billy, The Pretender, and The Wolf Brother are all incarnations
of the genius musician Will Oldham. I grew up swimming in West Point Lake, and this
poem references the Arthurian legend of the Lady of the Lake.

69.

the narrative not too painful but too mundane to be encyclopedic. here be ragtag esoterica.
the jagermeister must place the evergreen sprig in the dead buck's mouth to complete the kill.
to kill the albino buck will bring generations of curse upon your bloodline. now i sure know it.
bushmen chase the deer to death—Kalahari runners—we have beer bellies and rifles. arrows.
i have been lying to you for 705 lines now or have i? there's a creek in Sewanee that if you follow a
deer over it into the thicket you will become a deer yourself. our parents sent us to the far bank to
collect pocketknives, compasses, rifles, maps, wallets, deermusk & sunglasses dropped there.
we need more good gris-gris here. the Devil is vain; hang mirrors where you want to slow him.
do not follow the fifolet into the marsh. the treasure will be there in the morning. patience you.
don't count the fish while you are catching them or you'll catch no more that day. the narrative.

Notes

Jagermeister, in this poem, does not refer to the alcoholic beverage but to the translation
into "master hunter". The Kalahari runners mentioned in this poem refers to stories
of these hunters who run up next to the animal they are hunting and thus "scare" it
to death. The Sewanee Creek is a Tennessee waterway. A gris-gris is a voodoo amulet,
sometimes used for birth control. A Fifolet is a crewman buried with a pirate's treasure, to
guard it in spirit, and it can rise and walk the earth.

70.

i only knew you as the boy who got lynched but was good at math & your ghost was geometric.
the tree branches all hung with tethers which changed history & the trees were ashamed for us.
now golf-cart trails wind through woods as leaves fall. werewolves working the shopping malls.
flint, ash, sycamore, thistle, bear-oil, hickory, locust, cane staff. the tendons and sinews respected.
it's November. St. Hubert and the deer rut. he cured rabies, brought the hunt to church masses.
twelve-pointer striding up to us with rosaries and crucifixes in its antlers. killed it immediately. your
eco-poetry hieroglyphically spreading like moss and lichen over the downtown buildings.
let pregnant women put rusty nails in the garden to ensure the bountiful harvest. moon waxing.
hung the empty hornet's nest in the kitchen for luck. still were divorced. you re-married a wasp.
divorce means"to turn away"—as if walking out of Hades after looking back. as in salt pillared.

Notes

The Golf-cart trails in this poem are those in Peachtree City, Georgia—a town which can be completely traversed by this vehicle if need be. St. Hubert is the patron saint of hunters—he supposedly saw a crucifix hanging in the antlers of a deer in a vision—his Feast Day is November 3rd. Eco-poetry, according to Forrest Gander, is poetry "which investigates—both thematically and formally—the relationship between nature and culture, language and perception". Hanging a hornet's nest in a kitchen is supposedly good luck. The references to Orpheus and Hades refer to the poet's unsuccessful rescue mission of Eurydice.

71.

the Geiger counter goes clickety when you walk past the tent. we are coccyx deep in this project.
under the word CROATOAN was inscribed R'lyeh in Palmetto treetrunk. foolish hick teenagers.
you tickle a baby's feet it will develop a stutter. they cut the wings off Thelma's twisted ankles.
your hippocampus was named after a seahorse. olfaction of fresh conch. limbic sense of tides.
the verandas collapse into effluvium. the gardens splendor into conflagoration. no vendettas.
i was no Lapis Exilis. i just fell off the porch. full of ham and wine and whiskey. the fool again.
yet rising up just fine like the morning star to secure the rigging at the mooring of beginnings.
carving the sphinx in a bar of soap. carving the face of Alexander in an apple. it leathers well.
hummingbirds dueling with the dragonflies in the pagoda-light of the edenyard now bronzen.
deer being the moon herds being the Bacchic being the steeds of light being sustenance and arc.

Notes

A Geiger counter is a device used to detect radioactive emissions. The cryptic word
CROATOAN was a word, and a name of a Native American tribe, carved into a tree in
the camp of the lost Roanoke colony of North Carolina. R'lyeh is a lost city in the lore
of H.P. Lovecraft. The Palmetto Tree is a type of palm tree common in Florida and South
Carolina, for instance. Thelma was a waitress in Moreland, Georgia. The Lapis Exilis,
also considered the same thing as the Holy Grail by some, is a mystical stone which gives
the phoenix the power of rebirth. In regards to Alexander the Great and the riddle of
the Sphinx; I use this as a metaphor suggesting that the Greeks never truly understood
ancient Egyptian and other Eastern traditions. The Bacchic tradition refers to the
drunken and debaucherous worship of Bacchus.

72.

empanadas. funnel cake. cotton candy. deep-fried Snickers bars. diabetes with wings circling.
pingpong ball. fishbowl. catapults. balloon and darts. crossbow shoot. everything is rigged.
funhouse here from the kitchen to the bedroom. distortion in your hall-of-mirrors eyes. schism.
fanning the bonfire with a plastic dustpan roasting marshmallows on chicken bones. family.
everytime i listened to you snore in the recliner next to me with your Maker's Mark and oranges.
you were an authority on petroglyphs but couldn't change a diaper. derelict at church functions.
fishing wire taught around the garden hung with strategic Xmas ornaments. deer eat good here.
funhouse here from the bathroom to the back porch. you glaring and gleaming. my no remorse.
it's a $50,000 fine for hurting an amber snail. thus, Montezuma's treasure won't be unearthed.
& i have other get-out-of-matrimony schemes. lottery tickets. maps. robberies. forgeries. cons.

Notes

Maker's Mark is my mother's favorite drink, and she slurps it down while sucking on
sliced oranges. The Amber snail and Montezuma's treasure: in Kanab, Utah, the Aztec
treasure of Montezuma is supposedly hidden at Three Lakes, but excavating this area is
prohibited because it would harm the endangered snails.

73.

Papa Joe said it's cheaper to keep her. he says women sleep with who they want. men with who they
can. he says spoon her at least three times a week or someone else will keep the bed warm.
he says show me a beautiful woman and i'll show you a man who's sick of her shit. he was married
for 54 years. after Marvene died, he followed a few months later. all i ever wanted to
inherit was his boxes of arrowheads. he had taxidermied birds lying all over the house. a cuckoo
clock in the dining room. old piano covered in church hymnals. the carpenter's workshop where he
would make us wooden swords and shields and hatchets. many foxes grow grey but few grow good
said Benjamin Franklin. Papa Joe said man has his will but a woman has her way.
never marry a beautiful woman if you want to sleep at night. these old school buzzards, you got to
love them. the World War II men who raised us. the World War II women who reared us.

Notes

This poem consists of a lot of supposed "wisdom" passed down from Papa Joe regarding
women.

74.

banana spiders creeping about the front steps and beer cans behind hedge. grass needs cutting.
nights all like waiting in emergency room lobbies. in between tests. blood pressure off the charts.
Stretch Armstrong crucified to the live oak tree always disturbed me. neighbors' kids possessed.
hipster rich pseudo-lesbian sitcom babbles inane while preparing bowls of lemons and beersalt.
she said I watch Forensic Files to know how to get away with her murder. sip my beer quietly.
it's good luck for a virgin to piss on the fishing nets. we couldn't find one in ten counties. Cajuns.
once i knew i couldn't study at Crotona with Pythagoras i dropped out of Bowdon High School.
explains everything really. reading Prince Namor comics at Red's barbershop as men lamented.
banana spiders by back porch where the stray minx birthed her mangy kittens. feral green eyes.
question was not why couldn't you love one another. that's a stupid question. grow up already.

Notes

Banana spiders are hideous arachnids from Brazil. Stretch Armstrong was a toy
introduced in 1976. Forensic Files is a television program which presents crime scenes
and how investigators use them to track down culprits. Crotona was where Pythagoras
founded his mystical school. Bowdon High School is where I won Most Talented my
senior year for drawing. Prince Namor is a marvel comics character, and I used to read
these comics at my grandpa Red's barbershop.

75.

wandering sojourner stray mutt lab-mix saunters by drugstore panting or smiling with purpose.
life is confessing adultery to a priest who's philandering your wife. abdomen full of buckshot.
a group of rhinocerouses is called a crash. pahoehoe is smooth lava. i want to crash you on fire.
you won't buy antiques because they might have a demon yet you refuse to exorcise your own.
Tuscan, Doric, Ionic, Corinthian, Composite. Solomonic is particularly difficult. adult education.
your words and wounds daily crocheted into a cap for the newborn. you don't find this creepy?
you aren't Catherine of Aragorn. i will not behead anyone. still, i could cut out that liar's tongue.
i tried to get you to read Ron Silliman. i tried to read Ron Silliman to you. Ron Silliman on Mars.
now stray is climbing into the concrete culvert after something; he's whimpering. maybe rabid.
i didn't learn circular breathing for you. i didn't grow extra fingers and hands for you. megalo.

Notes

"Tuscan-Solomic" references different types of columns in masonry. Catherine of Aragorn was left by King Henry VIII for Anne Boleyn. Ron Silliman is an American poet and author of The Alphabet.

76.

increasing the frequency of gambling in that it decreases the probability of success.
increasing the gambling with frequencies until it increases maximum potentiality.
pushing one's luck like an old green Model T Ford Roadster on a mountain road.
parked outside of the motel beside her car knowing this is Roulette. driving away.

Notes

A Model T Ford Roadster was known as the first affordable automobile for the middle class—it's also known as the "Tin Lizzie". Roulette can refer to either a casino game or a game of chance which often ends in death by handgun.

77.

"He was born and raised around Jacksonville/ A nice young man not the kind to kill/
But the jealous fight and the flashing blades/ Sent him on the run through the everglades.
Running like the dog through the everglades". she was singing raspy and tapping her boot.
he was trying to fix the lawnmower again. he was going to lose two fingers on his strumming
hand. hand to mouth is how they lived, and it was good until it wasn't. he could smell him
all over the house. "Now the years went by and his girl was wed/ His family gave up they thought he
was dead/ Now and then the people would say/ They had seen him runnin' through the everglades/
Runnin' like a dog through the everglades". one time, Lee White almost burned down the barn. it
was the only time we'd seen Papa Joe cuss out and scream at Miss Marvene.
Lee White killed himself in high school. we think of this running through the dark woods.

Notes

The lyrics quoted throughout this poem are stolen from a song by the Kingston Trio,
written by Harlan Howard, called "Everglades". Lee White was a gradeschool friend of
mine who almost burned down my grandfather's woodshed, carpenter shop, and barn.

78.

burden laid down in the gospel sense. roof is repaired. new haircut. tooth pulled. holy for now.
Kepler died poor at 59 broke and fleeing religious countries, i told her. i was 38 and no genius.
musing on the stars under a mosquito canopy with Inez the guitar accompanying my heresies.
Steve, my mother's lover for over twenty years, told the story of driving from Georgia to N.Y.C.
with a load of ceramic floor tiles. black crew comes up to unload the truck in the Bronx. guy says
to Steve, "Where the fuck are you from?" Steve says "Georgia". guy looks at Steve for a minute,
says, "I wish you motherfuckers would've won that fucking war down there." a few guffaws.
in Kamakura, monks brought me saki on cliff's edge as it snowed. cherry blossoms shredding.
you may be born white trash in Alabama and end up on a promontory or vista over Kamakura.
it's because someone had to win some war or not. it's because you followed your destitute heart.

Notes

Johannes Kepler, a 17th century German mathematician and astronomer, died at 59.
Inez the guitar was the last acoustic guitar I owned and was last seen in the possession of
the poet, Charlie Farmer. Steve is my mother's boyfriend of over 20 years. Kamakura is a
coastal Japanese town known for its Buddhist and Shinto temple complexes.

79.

i wore Kavacha; i adorned Goshwit; i held Svalinn; i wielded Ichaival! your beauty matched all.
bested by tresses and the mole left of your full lips and the olive skin and dark Mayan eyes. God.
i never had a chance in the undersea caverns of you—mining the underworld wonders of you.
the quilt made with swaths of shirts and uniforms of our dead fathers and uncles was warmer.
the dark brown ceramic Buddha holding the seashell from Blackbeard Island. naturalistic lotus.
what will be packed in the seachest and put into deep storage with a padlock and my namecard?
we sat on backporch smoking the doobie talking about your divorce while i contemplated mine.
"Standing on the shoulders of giants/ Leaves me cold/ A mean idea to call my own/ A hundred
million birds fly away, away, away." those weren't leaves in the oaks they were crows, friend.
Talaria did not help me get away. Ellida was not fast enough. Vitthakalai also not fast enough.

Notes

A Kavacha is a mystical armor of Hindu legend which protects humans from harm
from the gods. Goshwhit is the helmet of King Arthur. The Svalinn is a legendary shield
from Norse mythology. Ichaival was a bow possessed by Odin which, once one arrow
was strung, it would shoot ten upon release. The Buddha holding a seashell is a spiritual
symbol for me and I have one in my office. Blackbeard Island is an amazing place to hunt
for seashells and sand dollars if you can avoid the park rangers. This poem contains lyrics
from the R.E.M. song "King of Birds". The Talaria are the winged sandals of Hermes. The
Ellida is the first Viking dragon ship. The Vitthakalai is the golden chariot of Kali.

80.

Vic Chesnutt, born in Zebulon, GA. Emily Dickinson pushing his wheelchair across Tarturus.
Ian Curtis is pushing Emily Dickinson's wheelchair across Elysium. Jeff Buckley dragging the river
with Ian Curtis' hanging rope trying to dredge up Elliot Smith. Kurt Cobain teaching Nick Drake
how to play southpaw. in the inherited recliner with skull candy headphones on pulsing.
it could take us all day to tune the drums. the humidity un-tuning our guitars. our fingers cut.
we were gonna take our grandfather's ghosts on tours of docked American haunted battleships.
a mapping of mysteries and mystics may not always save you. often it brings the quickening.
you remember honeysuckle not the poison ivy. the pristine wading pools, not the water-dogs.
does the quarry change for you when you learn how many have drowned in the lake? or not?
fat Baptist preacher keeps saying nobody dies they just meet punishments. he sweats bullets.

Notes

Vic Chesnutt was an American singer-songwriter, from Athens, Georgia, partially
paralyzed and confined to a wheelchair after a carwreck. Emily Dickinson was a famous
poet of American Romanticism. Tarturus was another realm of the dead, other than
Hades, in Greek mythology. Ian Curtis was the lead singer of the post-punk band, Joy
Division, who hung himself. Elysium, as mentioned elsewhere in the poems and notes,
was a paradise in the afterlife in Greek mythology. Jeff Buckley was an amazingly talented
singer/songwriter with the voice of an angel who drowned in the Mississippi. Elliot Smith
was an amazing singer/songwriter whose death was clouded in mystery. Kurt Cobain
committed suicide by shotgun, thus ending his songwriting career. Nick Drake was
another talented singer/songwriter who most likely died of an accidental overdose. A
southpaw is a left-handed boxer or a very cheap beer. Skull Candy headphones are my
preference for listening to indie-rock. Water-dogs are particularly viscious larvae of the
aquatic salamander.

81.

it was after the abduction that the town Moreland began to ostracize him. the doctors' gossiped.
it was like someone asked for rat poison at the pharmacy and then the whole town knew. Toby.
he didn't want to go to jail—they have the wrong kinds of bars in there. dumb luck counts too.
nueral clusterings like gravel alleyways in a town before first snowflake falls. all is ceremonial.
in dream of great-grandmother she turned to wipe flour on the apron but it was bloodred blood.
he saw the afterbirth of the universe pour out of the interdimensional cervix and went pinwheel.
they still looking for proof of a giant squid. it's like the lines that never got written by Rimbaud.
he thought Area 51 was where they kept geriatric huntsmen from accidentally shooting things.
lo and behold. tow & fold your hand. resolve and undermine. mow and sow gold. awe flowed.
hexes abundant. in pollen of the tigerlilies was the hexpollen. walked covered in this homeward.

Notes

Moreland, Georgia is where this book was primarily composed and where many of the stories are seated. Rat poison and Toby appear prominently in William Faulkner's short story, "A Rose For Emily". The quote, "They got the wrong kinda bars in there", was from the movie, Barfly—along with a quote from that movie which references, after a stabbing, that dumb luck counts too. The poem also refers to looking for proof of giant squids. Rimbaud was the revolutionary French poet who wrote Season In Hell. Area 51 is a government base which supposedly houses genetic monstrousities and alien technology.

82.

Cd was skipping. we were in the forest. Gander taking. a moonfield where a battle hated you so.
the roads we took were foundlings. the roads we took were orphans. the roads we took were.
my poetry professor talked about his inner reader. this entity knew words better than he could.
people used to say to me that i'm such a handful. handful of what i'd say. they'd shoot me birds.
you think couple of whacks to my guts is gonna get this good ol'boy down? no whitetrash shit.
hotter in here than two rats humping in a wool sock. and he is crazier than a sprayed roach.
he's acting like a three-legged dog in a meat-packing plant. maybe his head cutoff in an elevator.
either way, we recover from the mushrooms and eat at greasy spoon head to the record shops.
eagle took only parts of my liver & that lantern only burned off one hand. i'd do it all over again.
we took a gander at it. rode to D.C. to see Fugazi. yielded the battle at the craters of monuments.

Notes

C. D. Wright is an amazing American poet and was my teacher in Iowa. Forrest Gander is
an amazing American poet and was my teacher in Iowa. The Battlefield Where The Moon
Says I Love You was a book published by Lost Roads Press, by FrankStanford, which was
founded by C. D. Wright and Forrest Gander. While teaching, Forrest would often refer
to his "inner reader"—a part of him that interpreted the text differently. Line five is a
quote from the movie remake of Cape Fear, and I am quoting Robert De Niro. The eagle
and liver line is a reference to the myth of Prometheus. Fugazi is an amazing band—check
out their albums 13 Songs and Repeater.

83.

a cult was formed by the fire woman dancing in the smokestack lightning. the pastors kept lying.
we were glad they did because a world where the pastors told the truth would flip our evergrid.
all of us pushing wheelbarrows of our ancestors' body parts around to fertilze libraries of nihil.
"she makes you feel free and that's how it should be." all this time on your hands in dustbins.
he tried to explain to me redbone, high yellow, yellowbone. i got so pissed off I took his whiskey.
hitherto demonstrated numerous conclusions pertaining to the resistance which solids fracture.
Cherokee names falling like leaves all over this town. Cherokee names for everything reticent.
redbone cult. yellowbone cult. mulatto cult. children of the maize in trail of Oklahoma mazes.
the old 22-inch TV static the only light on in the room as the amp fuzzes and crackles with surge.
the liars kept pasteurizing. eugenics creeping through every hamburger. weed me out smiling.

Notes

The fire woman/smokestack lightning line references a song by the rock band The Cult—
"Smokestack Lightning" was also a song by the blues artist, Howlin' Wolf, and it refered
to sparks rising out of a chimney. There quoted lyricsare from the Ned's Atomic Dustbin
song, "Cut Up". Redbone, high yellow, and yellowbone are all slangterms for ethnic skin
tones.The eugenics in hamburgers final line in the stanza is a nod to conspiracy theories
involving engineered food, Nazi experiments, and Monsanto.

84.

good lord help me sweet baby jesus with mohawk and tambourine on a pogostick in a minefield.
when Cricket crashed a Chevrolet was how the story started but Cricket keeps earning his name.
always thought i'd name my daughter Acacia. flowers late winter. fruits in summer. Texan. no.
the thing is, ever since my Enoch moment, i can't name a thing. i sing it. i know it. cascadings.
people paying for IMAX experience for the ride at Vegas called the Magnificent Enoch Moment.
i just wanted to study physical geology & paleontology. dusting a different kind of chalk off me.
he'd bitch if you hung him with a new rope. that boy is 'bout as sharp as a cue ball. sawed-off.
he's riding a gravy train on biscuit wheels. don't let the door hit ya where the good lord split ya.
he's so god-damned ugly we tied a pork chop around his neck so the dogs would play with him.
ashes to ashes & dust to dust if it wasn't for women our parts would rust. bigot chaw spittle.

Notes

Cricket was an old black man from Lanett, Alabama who hung out at a sandwich kiosk
and was a wealth of local lore. Enoch supposedly lived for 365 years before he was
taken by God into the heavens. Acacias are short shrub-like trees also known as wattles.
IMAX theatres provide much more immersive movie or entertainment experiences and
supposedly have screens so large that there are no bad seats in the house.

85.

i found an un-marked grave inscripted with "sorry for the typos" & no date, birthright or name.
my den bigger with less cumbersome inherited chairs where less cumbersome poems were lithe.
which ten great books will you get buried with yourself? we set the limit ten for obvious reasons.
dropped in loveseats from B-52 bombers falling with magazines shredding towards that village.
i think Saturn's rings are metaphor of talking of gravity sure but of how our debris makes sense.
i want to sit in Papa Joe's chair once more instead of this interstellar console ergonomic bucket.
i worked a while marking moons for gods when i was a psychedelic guitarsmith of ample skill.
i was the H-bomb falling towards innocents and wanted to scream stop then i wailed oblivion.
the human animal will trample one of its species to death after a holiday for a flat bigscreen TV.
"if you have a daughter, bounce her on your knee; if you have a son, send the bastard off to sea"

Notes

B-52 bombers are mentioned particularly in this book as a reference to my grandfather
on my mother's side, Red. The H-Bomb, or atom bomb, was notoriously dropped on
Japanese cities during World War II. Saturn's rings are composed mainly of ice with a
little rocky material mixed in.

86.

loved tug-of-war. loved dodgeball. loved arcade. loved keg bounces. always loved wrong sports.
adage of death or taxes always made me laugh. it is death by taxes of course, Woodie Guthrie.
the Vodka i drank i snuck in this plush palace. have you ever done this? plush as velvet svelte?
my post card to you was from the least salt lake. the place you drivel away in with wife to sand.
salt. matrons turn into that when man walks away. i've noticed Sodom and Hades. pillars of silt.
my ex-lover only destroyed football teams with her wares and wiles. never anticipated poets.
palace was a vagina made of slot machines that had orgasms of tokens when you pleased them.
i never meant to be holy or bruised. never meant to be saavy or thug. just wanted a father's love.
a cruise is a heart valve. a moon mission is a transplant. i have always been a Martian. like you.
i liked it when the world was flat & we sailed off it listening to KANSAS while our parents slept.

Notes

Woodie Guthrie was an American folk muscician whose songs, primarily composed on
the guitar, were political and historical in nature. The band KANSAS has a famous song
known as "The Point of No Return", and the album cover is a ship going over a waterfall
ino a seemingly endless abyss.

87.

Guthrie-esque down tarred ribbons of highways. Johnny Appleseed-esque odalisque to Route 66.
i ain't whistlin' Dixie. i'd never whistle Dixie. spinning yarns—battening heddles and shuttles.
we went from moonshining to MDMA in less than a decade. from Willie Nelson to meth faster.
buddy-ro called these lines jeremiads. only Jeremiah i ever knew was all-state quarterback 1986.
falling on love is like being gored by a wild boar like Atys. like castrating Dionysus. not death.
i wondered if, on Mr. Williamson's land, a candidate for Apis existed. black, spotted with ritual.
sneaking into the kitchen at night after the preserves had set to drink the vinegar from the jars.
skulking behind a pool table in that seventies' mist was your dark hero in a ghostly wife-beater.
you may have been born from good stock but someone spilled the cursed pot. stowaway mick.
they keep making most of us on conveyor belts to go and die in desert wars for dead dinosaurs.

Notes

Johnny Appleseed was a tinpan hat wearing wanderer who planted apple trees, according
to legend, all over America. "Whistlin' Dixie" is a term which means wasting time.
The term jeremiad, derives from the weeping prophet, Jeremiah. Route 66 is legendary
and one of the first highways which crossed America. MDMA, also known as molly, is
3,4-Methylenedioxymethamphetamine, the psychotropic compound. Willie Nelson is
a country music musician and marijuana enthusiast. Atys was the Greek Eunuch god
castrated by a wild boar. Dionysus was the Greek god of wine and revelry. Apis is the
name of many possible ancient Greek kings, prophets, or healers.

88.

surrounded the bonfire with thousands of lunatic candyskull bobbleheads. watched them laugh.
2.25 kilos healthy plums. 1.35 kilos of sugar. 1 gallon water. 1 tsp. lemon juice. wine yeast. jugs.
the summer party will result in four pregnancies, ten fights, three arrests, and one parapelegic.
the whole small town written by Frank Miller and filmed by Darren Aronovsky. starring you.
there were no jobs for pickpockets after the textile factories co-opted to Africa, India, Indochina.
die old and leave a manageable orca. the boy wanted to climb every water tower he ever saw.
bouquets by bad curves. bouquets by traintracks. bouquets random. cumulonimbus bouquets.
a soul out of a body. it's like a mirror near you when you are fucking that you refuse to look at.
if the freedom of information act was applied to this town then gates of hell would chew it up.
i would sincerely hope so. she should keep the baby. we should go. call if you need anything.

Notes

Frank Miller is a Gothic noir-inspired writer of films and graphic novels. Darren
Aronovsky is a writer nd director of what are considered deeply disturbing and
controversial films by mainstream American culture. The Freedom Of Information Act
contains at least nine exemptions based on government restrictions to the general public
reading about its government's activities.

89.

dollarstore toys. wooden clothespins. junk drawer paper-clip swords for cheap commandos.
everything bad between men and women is written in motor oil, mascara, spermicide, and rum.
you don't know your town until they drag the river and Shep Hardy knows how to scuba-dive.
everyone ran towards the ice cream truck but i just waited by the mailbox. a sense of inevitable.
assholes felt like outlaws but were just hipsters who got out of credit card debt. loathing foam.
ashes of outlaws were stock of the bisque of the mayor's brit milah which got him twice elected.
secret handshake. do you feel honor with that? do you feel power with that? two switchblades.
they say write what you know but in the tornado alley trailerpark you don't get to know much.
they are afraid i can see into them. they brought on the dancing horses. i handicapped them.
one night he made us grab a basketball pole & beat us into submission. i never went to the prom.

Notes

Shep Hardy was a gangster who barely avoided getting nabbed by the Texas Rangers.
A brit milah is a Jewish circumcision ritual. There is a reference to an Echo and the
Bunnymen song in line nine of the poem. An ice-cream truck once drove through your
neighborhood selling Drumsticks. Tornado Alley is a term, meteorologically speaking, for
the region of the United States where tornadoes are the most common.

90.

the American flag is a slit wrist and the wind makes it bleed so much that purple is sky chrome.
i am slanted and enchanted and disenfranchised & romantic and septic and running back. gore.
i will sail the Pequod back to the flat end of the earth and do a Niagra please to stop colonialism.
stop fretting over execration. your mark of Cain was a skagtag tat above your asscrack. pleeze.
got drugs in Slidell. crossed Lake Pontchartrain. sold them to the fratboys all night. sinisterly.
Greyhound back to college. started a punk band. got accepted to MFA program. went bankrupt.
Immanuel Kant never travelled more than ten miles from his boyhood home. didn't work for me.
the America flag is a thin-lipped chartreuse with too much foundation on too many blue bruises.
never went back to Slidell. old hotel flophouse is now corporate stripmall i am told by heathens.
the American flag is a red wound with pale pus seeping from it & blue infection veins spidering.

Notes

The Pequod was the ill-fated ship of Captain Ahab in Moby Dick. The Mark of Cain was put on him by God so that no one would kill him in his exile. A skagtag is a slang-term for a tattoo on the small of someone's back. Slidell, LA is across Lake Pontchartrain from New Orleans and was a known crime zone when I stayed there briefly. Immanuel Kant was an influential Enlightenment philosopher who never married and supposedly never traveled more than 10 miles from his home.

91.

heave and hollow of infant's chest in TV static glow as curtains murmur with summer whispers.
you always said you would never procreate just fornicate and now your blood sussurates anew.
her breaths so infrasonic you fear she left this world. there are eyes on the tips of the starfish.
the old Fender bass leans in the corner by the crib and the diaper bin looks like R2-D2's cousin.
the feral kittens sleep under the porch endangered by armadillos. owls chortle in the magnolias.
you have become something greater now. you have become something less now in her powers.
giant Cherokee beings stretch their consciousness across the skies above your cottage with lore.
the redtail hawks sleep with their beaks in their wingpits and the corn wilts in quiet darkenings.
they're aren't even any family portraits on the walls yet & y'all aren't exactly newlyweds either.
heave and hollow of infant's chest as the sun warms the curtains. you've stared at her all night.

Notes

The Fender Bass was played by John Entwistle of the rock band The Who. R2D2 is a
famous droid from the Star Wars mythos.

92.

West Point Lake was high fed by the Chattahoochee. Papa Joe says "Atlanta flushed its toilets."
cotton mills shut down to go to sweatshops elsewhere but Koreans brought in the KIA plants.
Old Man Padgett got hung by the man he meant to hang at Starr's Mill. ghost hunters go there.
these towns named after the Marquis de Lafayette. the fay one. the fey one. the Enlightenment.
ley lines running under our home which once was a church connecting us to lodge, jail, banks.
they're eight points on a Maltese cross. Amalfi. the Hospitaller. Oak Island treasures. cursed.
Observant. Tactful. Resourceful. Dexterous. Explicit. Discriminating. Persevering. Sympathetic.
y'all tired yet? hell no! y'all tired yet? hell no! y'all wanna go? hell no! wanna stay? hell yeah!
good Korean food, jobs. Lanett, Alabama. its methnicities. Asian rednecks. country Confucians.
Papa Joe said my ear problems probably came from swimming in the Chattahoochee. The Hooch.

Notes

West Point Lake is referenced many times in this book—in this context it is because of
how polluted it became by the time I was an adult. The KIA Plant in Lagrange, Georgia
brought new industry to the collapsed textile industry of Lanett, West Point, etc. The
Marquis de LaFayette was a mystic and soldier and he has many cities, landmarks, roads,
and destinations named after him in America. The Chattahoochee River is the natural
border between Alabama and Georgia and between the towns of Lanett and West Point
where I spent my childhood. This passage also refers to the Starr's Mill/Old Man Padgett
Ghost Story in Senoia, Georgia. The Maltese Cross, Amalfi, Hospitaller, etc. all refer to
the order of medieval knights who became the house of Malta. Oak Island, near Nova
Scotia, supposedly hides ancient Knights Templar treasure. Observant-Sympathetic refer
to the observations of those who follow the Maltese Cross.

93.

everything you read has immense value. everything forgot has immense value. you die a library.
read more than write. always. listen more than you sing. always. inscribe stone when it's time.
i fantasized i'd be co-opted by a black helicopter but now i know it's by amateur drone hobbyists.
William Blake on his back looking up into that tree and seeing the angelic and acid-engraving it.
Illuminated Printing invented. now your turn. of course you are soldiering the great singularity.
intaglio. no relief in these relief etchings. repoussage. stylus. copper plates. hit back of the plate.
i have to write twenty bad poems to get one good line. wish i could hammer them from the back.
village fool taught himself to write backwards in mirrors but was called autistic. short-sighted.
i was born with and surrounded by and terrorized by libraries i would never dowse for treasure.
when called smart, should be insulted. put smart back in the basket or else it gets the hose again.

Notes

Black helicopters are supposed government surveillance vehicles but we know they have
all been replaced by drones. William Blake, a Romantic poet, invented the incredible
art of Illuminated Painting/Printing in only the way that a one of a kind genius like
him could. A repoussage is a metalworking technique in which a malleable metal is
ornamented or shaped by hammering from the reverse side to create a design in low relief.
The last line of the poem references a horrifying scene from the film Silence of the Lambs.

94.

wonder how many names my parents considered before naming me & you don't you? Archibald.
hex on the nexus or sextant towards vortex or a place for a good rest or the philosopher's stone.
there is emerald in all of us. moonstone too. i broke a hematite horse once. became suspicious.
Beaucephalus. the Black Stallion movie. one where the boy almost drowns. and the darkhorse.
i wish i could whisper around a great bonfire to all of the heroes who once rode black stallions.
bonfires of us screaming in cities under the underworld in cities beneather than sin. grim torque.
the torch you wield or weld is cauterizing the wounds of oil tycoons makes me giggle and gurgle.
wonder how many corporations were named after the continents that they mined? sinister shit.
next on the plank? sextexting for hedge-funds? platinum mines & trillium. Africa, Africa, Africa.
Archibald implies that you are one who wants to archive or understand rivers of immense tomes.

Notes

The meaning of the name "Archibald" means precious and bold. Beaucphalus was
Alexander the Great's horse. Sexting is texting explicitly erotic things to someone from
your cellphone. Hematite is a black mineral which can be very brittle—I once had a small
hematite stallion carving which I dropped and broke on the sidewalk. The Black Stallion
was a movie, circa 1979, which I associate with Alexander and his horse.

95.

psychomachia of kitchen table. the lacustrine hardwood floors of beer, piss, and tears. evenings.
when the weather balloon crashed, pieces we found could be wadded up & would fold back out.
triangle peg game says i'm a genius. Magic 8-Ball says so too. fortune cookie says i am victorious.
milk jugs hang from maples. fishing wire around garden perimeter. too many banana peppers.
Manius Aquillius killed, having molten gold poured down his throat. i'm dying likewise burned.
record skipping like the heart murmur that would kill her later as she crochets Laertes'pajamas.
militia groups reveling at their barbecues and gunshows. survivalists sojourn in their bunkers.
the great deluge of data surging through our membranes unfettered in its psychomachian tryst.
you could get shot real quick in that household for losing the remote or not emptying spittoons.
all i could see was the whitetail but i followed it down a dark pathway into utter primeval black.

Notes

A Psychomachia is the conflict between the soul and the body. A Magic 8 Ball is a toy for
random generation of possibilities using a liquid solution and a geometric solid. Laertes
was the father of Odysseus. The word lacustrine means anything associated with lakes.
Manius Auillius was executed by having molten gold poured down his throat.

96.

under hypnosis he still spoke in tongues. there was no way to diagnose the demons of hillbillies.
campfires surrounded by melungeons. partus sequitur ventrem. can't assimilate in these parts.
dismantled our drag cars to build a Trojan keg to get into their city hall. Judge Laocoon wailed.
we traveled cross-country to Yoknapatawpha County. nothing was the same as we had left it.
homespun downhome plainspoken quips. i still don't ever believe Papa Joe about the mermaids.
the thought of retribution painfully slow like a centipede tedious across worn carpet. yearning.
i thought it was turtle shell turned out to be skull. watched the sunset and mushrooms sprouted.
could have been a rocket scientist but he became the best taxidermist Lanett, Alabama ever had.
greatest epic singer born from family that never understood a word of my song. neo-Hart Crane.
they have only found ten haplocantosauruses. they call this rare. you laugh and call it precious.

Notes

Speaking in tongues is the act of "getting the spirit" and spontaneously verbalizing in a
church setting. "Partus sequitur ventrum" means "the offspring follows the mother"—
thus many are born into slavery. Yoknapatawpha County was created by William Faulkner
in order to be populated by his genius fction. Melugeons are dark-skinned peoples,
supposedly descended from the Portuguese, who settled in the Tennessee mountains.
Laocoon was trying to expose the Trojan "keg" when he was killed by serpents, along with
his two sons. Hart Crane is one of the most beautiful American poets ever, but he threw
himself into the ocean.

97.

what do you call 1,000 lines set upon to finish the hunt of a white stag? what better quest word?
Ursula K. Le Guin did this to me. Ursula of the pond. Ursula of the forest. Ursula you little bear.
all i have learned of the constellations helps me not in making better love to this Ishtar Kali-Ma.
what do you call 1,000 times towards the narthex of the temple with offerings too simple to fruit?
i floated and bounced and plagiarized and forged and laundered and embezelled all your checks.
flannel brings you musing on some Scotch origin you can't remember you drunken glad wench.
always getting stabbed at night by pens you fall asleep with and bruised by the notebooks too.
i love you not enough to follow you to hell. said i would have to shepherd the goats to Elysium.
always thought my spirit-animal was a koala. nursing a cold with terrible claws. you disagreed.
1,000 lines called you like a murder of crows from the trees shredding clouds like cotton candy.

Notes

Ursula K. LeGuin was a fantasy and science fiction author whose last name means "little bear". The White Stag was a mythic retelling of the history of the Huns and the life of Atilla, written by Kate Seredy. Ishtar is the Sumerian fertility goddess. Kali Ma is the Hindu goddess of creation, preservation, and destruction known as the "Dark Mother".

98.

running about this small town with easel in your hand never knowing where to plant it. where to start. camera-men running behind you and your easel constantly sending the Cloud your meanderings. drones buzzing behind the camera-men chasing them chasing you filming the filmers while other painter paints all all of it with Sigmar Polke directing the lighting & emulsion fluids. rather die on a bone in a catfish joint than for jihad. die a poor painter. not to ever live forever. rather, he was eaten by a giant catfish while diving to set explosive charges for West Point Dam. Hiawatha, not Jonah. "this place is like a reliquary of discretions past". in the pork belly of it all. Hiawatha, never Noah. she is the outrigger and she guides you through dire tempest, your Hina. diving down into the dark with the knife between my teeth hoping they are painting and filming. thought he was an albino but Cricket came home covered in chalk of a thousand bad classes.

Notes

"The Cloud" is simply slang for a network of servers whose function is to store data for various personal and public purposes. Sigmar Polke was an experimental German photographer, multi-media artist, and painter. West Point Dam created West Point Lake near the town of Lanett which many of these poems reference. Hiawatha was a legendary Mohawk warrior, and he is connected to the canoe and water myths. Jonah was a Biblical prophet famous for being swallowed by a fish. Noah was a Biblical patriarch who survived The Great Deluge. Hina, according to Iwi mythos, was a matriarchal goddess who was violated by the Eel God.

99.

in terms of scrolls, postulates, portents, torrents, postscripts, archivings—this body was a vessel.
a direct correspondence between technology, blood sugar, alchohol, and mysticism required.
i took myself apart in terms of ships to make a horse full of seed to enter the city of her awesome.
then we were attacked by one-eyed napalm-clad things of fire and alchemical purity we loved.
then we had to go home & drive tractors over continents of the dead and the memories of them.
horror is not going to war & horror is coming home from war & horror is winning a fucking war.
Jim Morrison said that violence isn't evil—that the infatuation with violence is evil. cornshuck it.
war is going to glamour. war's suckling, a celebrity. war is a nuclear bomb neglige. war hungry.
every time a building burned down or was excavated or was demolitioned i saw fathers' faces.
the best we can do is make better okra from the ashes and better molasses. we learn to glisten.

Notes

Jim Morrison was a rock singer and poet and the frontman for the group The Doors.

100.

the balconies and verandas now all covered in the ivy from the spilt vendettas. suitors can climb.
truckerslang behind the greasy spoon overheard regardless of motorcycles revving incessantly.
somewhere in Karnak in a parallel dimension beyond the great paradox i have responsibilities.
no one here ever lets truth get in the way of a good boring. no one wants a tour of your tit-town.
we now had the killswitch in wristwatches capable of incinerating our childhood imaginations.
dream of having a hot air balloon which could have flown over the ancient monuments thriving.
i accidentally victoriously remember part of gestation inside my mother when i was a seahorse.
what is read what is channeled what's written what's sampled what's indoctrinated what's lyric?
was this one place in Carrollton, Georgia where i devoured best carne asada of my life. seriously.
i woke with a shovel in the bed. wife texting. daughters with telescopes. time to live. strangely.

Notes

"truckerslang"—the language of truckers—for example, Tampa, FL is known as "Cigar
City" and an "alligator" is a blown tire in the road. Karnak—an ancient Egyptian temple
complex which I gained knowledge of through Marvel Comics. Carollton, GA—this
town is the home of the University of West Georgia where I attended West Georgia
College as an under-graduate before it became a major university in the state. I can't recall
the name of the restaurant where I found the carne asada, and it no longer exists.

The Morphnacular

morphnacular i. : anagnorisis

O onion-skinned epic   there is always a woman yet
        this misleading thread   asthmatics with scuba gear
by this river we could camp here or bilge it   i'm frakkin
        solipsistic over it   crafting forevers in these fevers
affixed to the apogee   good goddamned wrecked racked reekage
        the overcast of shattering as-is   this is not meant to be
apocalyptic   or to make you asthmatic   banners
        hanging from stoplights plastic cries of seagulls
by the skeleton key tchotchke factories   whooping by the wharves
        junk-drawers splinteress   splendor of tripe afterglow
earplugs, paperclips, rubber bands, your hospital bracelets
        the silos of refuse in orbit   the signals bouncing
back to us from their pulpits   nubile nebulae spilling
        procreative bacteria-rich dust   I can't even roll down
the window in this forecasted effluvial my nodes throbbing
        rhumba towards a waterfall in a rainstorm or in other
words overload but not a lie   unless one is caught
        with his thumbdrive in the cookies there
eyes flung upwards like poised scythes   prayers like sutures
        but the inflection is untreatable   beings becoming been
histories' burps and/or formulae -epic O-face   eclipse of you

...

morphnacular ii. : Bono postcard hamartia

got the key to the city   kismet left immediately   felt like porn
         or worse a jetlagged lolly-gagger in a daisy-chaingang
bought an albino alligator skin jacket   charged a cardinal's
        kibitzing on a stolen identity   at the audit I paid dearly
Hysterica the best country   no one ever had to work again
        meant to be metaphorical and still made millions
with a mullet to boot   brought back the breadbox full of vacci-
        nations of the lotus and breadfruit and cassava
and the vagrants and immigrants full of affidavits   forging checks
        in the sweatshops   spillproof holy grails
slick as a shark's moustache   Amsterdam and balderdash
        skin biopsies no issue under the scalar wave
facilities churning the ionosphere with policies   the casino inside me
        the slot-machine tongues of my treaties   I'm a snowplow
that causes summer   always a geyser   they show movies
           on my incisors   your days are surely encumbered

...

morphnacular iii. : bus-ride peripeteia

lullabies plucked   spear-chucked   into moonlanding
          old bike tied to an oak in front of the methadone clinic
obese tie-dye boards transit by fleetfox anorexic   all designer
          soundtracked   your whole life was heretofore a dollar store
dooby druthers song   a caravan of ants tours the vista next
          Japanese cameras exploding with indie rock all over the plaza
still-life's: "sky with unpaid bill"   "wheelchair in carwreck"
          "turban fights skullcap by beehive near mohawk"
following art-school girls to the commissary   applying
          for the job at the Band-Aid factory   naval officer
in movie threatened the top gun that he'd end up flying rubber shit
          cargo planes   sounds like gainful aeronautics to me
drangstrum   paronomasia of textslang like eoliths, we once
          thought our poems were on purpose   it's been un-erfed
like eoliths   that these rhymes you be stealing is naturally-occurring
boregasm ensues   at the stop pull the cable's nerve
revengicide on this citadel tonight
gonna show the heart I got left

                    . . .

morphnacular iv. : aporia of Saturday night

infinitives shackled   story as we've erased it   moss and lichen
          cryptic etch and skewered   gotharabesque
hymenopteran surveillance above this juxtajunta   no rustic to run to
          wheezing across this floodplain   walking enneagram
we just can't lose   it's onomerican   gosu, habu, or chobo
          all in the same bloat together   cinemerican
members of MENSA on heroin   they were bar-tossed lovers
          parachute shreds for handkerchiefs for these polyurethane
tears sold on the lack market   don't tase me bro
          the vajazzled skyline with the Adderalled el trains
let's lie here in the crater we made when we fell from eight miles
          magnetar amphetamine zipper   your wiseacreage
and bravado   I imagine you naked in a field of goldenrod
          you claimed to be Jalamity Cane   I laughed cash
whatnots littered the wind with sweet butterfly silt
          cap the flask of the epoch   if-icate tonight's ions
walking out of the icestorm   the word made of me
          thief, bulimic, whore, cannibal, god, worm
process and procession of them   but I indie-rocked out
          of that   a tiara of chakras every day is chewing thru
a hanged man's noose   we won't always be able to barrel roll
          malaise out of everything   cryptosymbiosis moss and lichen

                              . . .

morphnacular v. : zeitgeist parallax

my tongue paraplegic trapeze artist   neverendum chainlink lyric
        cosmogony with missing memes   the lease on this species
in foreclosure   scrapyard of zombie preparedness   third-eye
        is my hot air balloon   migraine of Dasein though
umbra of summer   this world so crepuscular arcanamurica
        laptop lexicon of shopping spasms   data-Bedouin
the lepidoptery of synapses   electric eels of verbs about
        the weather vanes of nouns   time to let the laurels rain
hollow tetragrammaton of orb on which we slack   smithsonionize these mutants
        jawbone icon held up to lightning storms at foot of Kubrick monolith
if only grace were a widespread plague   epipha-knots in bubble chambers
        nation suffering from nocturnal teeth-grinding   fleshpots
should realize the road to wisdom leads to the malice of coliseum
        vibrantly violent violins for the vagaries   does everything
really have to be a product of ancient aliens?   were we not designed
        to be the arctic cosmic slingstone slag of time-travelling gods?
i'll hang myself from the tallest laughters   mark your poetics
        on the blowgun with the woodburner and tranquilize a scion
something to believe in   hunchback economy wades down the Mississippi
        kyriarchy and eleison down the node that i must
nano

. . .

morphnacular vi. : anunnaki dysphemism

 join in the gestalt the data
            basalt, up to bonelevel
mercury notwithstanding
            all us steeplechased into
stun-gun barricades
            scratch a ticket at the petrol
station of riding a bullet
            into the founding father's
liquor cabinet and just desire
            to walk on the moon made
us beautiful—then, we had
            to go and do it—this whole
thing was a dare to monadic
            overdrive—we didn't even
know until the bit was pulled
            out of our mouths how to
say extraterrestrial

                         . . .

morphnacular vii. : midlife hypophora

life begins like a flight to Vegas
          gambling themes metastasized
you find ideologies quicker than
          your hotel keys—midlife
you look down flying over the salt lakes
          a junkyard of misgivings
under your Sopwith Pegasus
          your purchases exploding
like pigeons over rooftops
          you are hired to be a navigator
of hemorrhages, images of western
          ruin, relic, anything racemiferous
oxymoronic oxy addict with a lifespan
          wider than the mythology's
wingspan and that thunderbird flew
          centuries before the mesas were named
after dead shamans, pueblos, & petroglyphs

                              . . .

morphnacular viii. : homo sapiens sapiens meiosis

cardiac   like a frozen metronome
          cataract   like a tusk in an iceberg
aching swoon after swoon after swoon
          of Linnaeus-lineage   of Loki-kin
a Prometheus-prima donna   prankster in
          the viscera of the schemata
up to civilization all along   cuneiform
          dripping its triangles from your sacrificial
wounds   subliminal in boxes of breakfast
          cereals and action figures with their
conspiracy iconography   call them crazy
          the demi-surge coursing through suburbs
trying to keep the party below cop level
          but dirty bombs and biological noirfare
i'm really not vibing your microcosmos,
          man—sign your sine-curve away
like a melting iceberg   the dose too late

                    . . .

morphnacular ix. : cubicle snark solecism

shank, shave, shirts, shit, rank and file
            endless alliterations of illiterates, days
replicating pixilation   no simpatico
            galumphing through hoops ablazen
frame, quadrant, quartered, drawn into quatrains
            the pretzel bun is back it's lunchwagon
fold the ace flush gamol in imaginary sfumato
            and you got to haggle the super-model
this was all swiveling in your ergonomic chair
            when you got there   it's not your haute
don't let them see that John Ashbery book
            in your desk drawer   there is a hitman
coming for you no worries, no worries
            your hobocore backhomies will read
your elegies   then they will be made into
            a terra cotta army to protect you
in your illustrious luminous corporate afterlife

                                    . . .

morphnacular x. : golden age paraprosdokian

the lightning bolt the strep-throat the three steins containing destiny
the rigamarole the diastole the lore of the legion of generation latchkey

the reasons the chapels are locked at night the column of iconic arête
the squalor the train's holler the alarming despondent discrepancies

the tin cans the middlemen drooling albumen the battleship-bolt factories
Hecate spread wide like a matrix on a mattress the secret manuscripts

trying to straddle the evening on burning eaves of past amendments
night after night getting lit up like gold becoming lead like solar to saturnine

the flare-guns all firing above the posh plush homes of the one-party-ticians
epithets of new physics at odds with a godhead of wordsmiths lyric scientists

Baudrillard said we'd never defeat the system on the plane of the real sphere
mapping atoms and genomes and deconstructing atoms and genomes and

cycloptic we are all wunderkind thriving with nacreous floraciousness
the concords all glitched with interdimensional travel apparitions and apparatus

in the fiber optic cumulostratus and the drone nucleus sporing simultaneously
but the work is never lost upon us, oh no, more hybrids, cryptids, and chimeras

to be toggled—stay wanton—we have anaphasia of idiot luck—we lustrous

...

morphnacular xi. : Empedocles and the apis

prolegomenon shattered   the threshold
           icon genomes   mandalas that will cut you
quark soup   amphibian emergence
           to escape Disney swastikas   to evol
call a linguist, a botanist, an ornithologist, and
           an ichthyologist to survive this craven
dystopia discordium   suture slumerica
           aerate it like worms in paradisic soil
figs rotting in the fridge   snakeskin boots
           under the elm   poor swagmen
so selenography leads to documentation of ocelli
           divine geometer   fertile crescent banks
hover in the modicum   genome mandalas
           bantam drums and oil spills
we are all girls in the gutters when the comets
           come down with their ides for our
      Kentucky-fried towns   we all got billy-clubbed
nihil-post-avantists; maybe there's a bonus round
mitochondria clutching to the wheels
of a Mars rover   amera-seraphim microbial
           write on the soon to be bombed
walls of the never sacred wombs with paranoid
           hieroglyphs   mystic analog is now
digital cyber-fraud   quantum physics, though
           can't discern a woman's laugh

                                    . . .

morphnacular xii. : Lacanian mutatis mutantis

i imagine you had a carwreck with god   i imagine
the houseplant is cosmic to you   i imagine
you thought you wrote "Kubla Khan"   i xanadu
you walking away from a landslide you
caused in the planetarium   trailer-parks in
hurricane lane never heard of you, i imagine
why complain of the tridents or avalanches?
you are a used-car salesman   i indoctrine
you swimming through an Alabama graveyard
dontja dontja? the waboosh template
four bubbles just swam up my beer bottle
so dissident   let's snowboard across
a wave of ashen bones   mass graves
of theorems of plastic halls of masks
mainly the helmets of hazmat I imagine you
prog you   buzz you   punk you
soft as a maggot   hard as a coffin nail
psychonaut in a backwash hydroplane
you have major sinthomes   i imagine your
mirror   it's a screaming cicada swarm
ancient sonar of the owl its head swiveling the
other/other   a compass in an armoire
never touched a compact and a lipstick
never opened sea glass on a bathroom
saucer   you, Freudian on the toilet

...

morphnacular xiii.: Axis of Andriambahomanana

i fed you myths and nothing astonishing came out.
you wiped honey off your lips telling me to play better lyre.
no, we can't copulate with the maker's harems. vile loper.
eater of apples of the nubiles' nipples. souls hanging on our windchimes.
bent needle and burnt bottlecap by the poppy field. you are falling man.
you are falling, man. carried by the crow across scarecrow vegas.
omenic revelatories.   harvesting a wicker world by active volcanoes.
lonely ark myth disintegrating. pundits scramble virtuoso. wordwarps
keep the populace copacetic in innuendo. if only the world was a free
barbecue. all are autumn-glad. all are instant grams of irony-clad.
red hair of ancient dispellings from crystal palaces the blue blood
spilled into the water supplies. agape is no pulsating octopus; it's
not even a unicorn-pegasus. cloudshape history on its nape of whim.
clouds are dirt and water. just like us, i told you. what's the use—
you saw that horizon and needed to lay your spear flat across it.

. . .

morphnacular xiv.: Albuquerque waffle house hodoiporeo

the inevitable themes   idioms in the void
      it takes a lot of equipment to know what equip-
meant needs to be fitted with   eureka!
      the arctic place of first emulsion   equip.
marsh and masthead   cave and catacomb
      coal and crystal   ash and hecatomb   tome
of undead seas   it's not our medicine frequencies
      a note. a key. askew.   something's beneath
the brake can't push it down kind of feeling is
      always the weather   rag and bone man philo-
mass-amnesia   honey is the only food that never rots
      and the drones are searching the 'hoods for it
rafferty rules galore   universities of satyromania!
      cops lining the road like alligator alley
the entire landscape tastes like fried chicken skin
      a century sweating out the bends and dementia tremens
used a phoenix for a zippo   cowboyrica
      roadtrip of descending   Schrödinger's dashboard
compartment of contraband vs. walls of borderguard moustaches
      removed the clock tumors made cheeseburgers
everyone posted bail   outside the Georgia O'Keefe museum
      orchids wiping thieves' gold off our lips
freedom or passage for naught   just melting the modicum
      with this transmission   trailblazin' off the pier

...

morphnacular xv.: choroplethic hypsometric isopleth

atlas of whims   atlas of sweet nothings
         atlas of burned dinners   atlas of birdshit fractals
atlas of unfinished manifestoes   atlas of broken woodwinds
         atlas of shattered glass objects   atlas of shrugs
atlas of discarded doors   atlas of discarded tat ideas
         atlas of times you almost met Donald Sutherland
no poverty is greater than the loss of an event horizon
         atlas of ginger supermodels   atlas of bathrobes
atlas of shini sou   atlas of broken hammers   atlas of unfs
         atlas of nautili   atlas of spiracles   atlas of nerf
atlas of steampunk aircraft   atlas of splinters
         atlas of asshole art curators   atlas of animal spines
atlas of minefields   atlas of pine needles   atlas of boll weevils
no poverty is greater than the loss of an event horizon
         we are taller than crestfallen   bolder than aldermen
unleashing implosions for the cosmic Ponzi
         investing in wonderment so sticky your fingers become it
atlas of thoughts you were yet to have   pages torn out of it
         atlas of torn out pages   atlas of famous forewords
atlas of awesome indexes   atlas of famous last words
         no poverty is greater than the loss of an event horizon

. . .

morphnacular xvi: scratch-ticket hypostasization

and the only way out of any of it was to hit the Powerball
        so many of them scratched and guess one gets tendonitis
victims of spleen and fortune   rolling in waxen placards
        of nicotine and fast food seasons   what happens
when an immovable compendium meets an unstoppable
        effluvium?   snowcone stands and heavy exhales
I told The Flood that it did not precipitate nearly enough
        cinema-miasma of the American moviescope
gila monster toxic romance of western gangster sploitation
        a pagoda of railroad spikes criss-crossed on windowsill
as a testament to illegal trespassings and past roadtrips
        we cut out the tongues of manifest destiny   vigilantes
eating bacon in bedbug-ridden hovels typing contracts
        for regimes paid for by telemarketing execs but we still
had our Moleskines!   pathetic wretches   who never knew
        a wartime economy   the third world mining the conductors
for our cellphone efficiencies   right the word flight 100
        more times with the oil on the end of the broken wing
tricked the wasps and starlets into attacking by wearing
        a toolbelt of impossibilities   they love staying unfinished
every rose has its Oxycontin   the sweat lodge and the secret
        handshake and the stag lodge and the long lodge and
the secret jailbreak of the muckrakers for el presidente's sake
        we became angered that the martyrs had used our sins
as a way to leave this world and travel the dimensions
        the future us   all shaped like wineglasses   slender
receptacles with the CPU floating in cybernetic fluid

...

morphnacular xvii: perlecutionary act of denizens

saga of exile, no sequel   evol of apathetic nada
    eschew and shed the layered nautilus swirls
the S's in the dollar signatures   the whispers in the churned
    topsoil where the exiled tries to climb back into
prominence of stained-glass window gets cut to holy pieces
    destinies clinging to olives in cocktails
roots of trees throbbing under humming duplexes   carnal
    is it the lack of noblesse which makes me so digress?
all of us   ebony nebuchadnezzars   on a pilgrimage for wanton
    altogether, all flings retrograde   our werewolves
all shaving in greasy spoon bathrooms to emerge as
    debaucherous senators of Americanly average Saturdays
we always chose cavern not tavern   and hid behind belvederes
    your dead mother's spine for a walking stick
and the grandfather's scrapbook for a cerebral cortex
    snowglobes full of bedhead dread lining the mantles
I'll dance at your shredding   no flurries   all will be
    fair to middlin'   I was more afraid of the needle
than bedlam   we stole   Ebola from Arcadia
    and lamented the complaints of the newly risen
you never sent the postcards but you tattooed the postscript
    hummingbirds flew from the hive of our arguments
men ran into the milky sky from the tops of tenements
    loose change falling from their pockets
into piggybank aps   up the embankment of the melted
    scrapmetal symbols to find our mettle
mockumentary producers   peddling maya and mantras
    holograms of our former selves paid as extras

. . .

morphnacular xviii: universal instantiation of mass charlantanism

we all hang-glided to work to get our bonuses
        we plunged our afflictions into pillowcases
to dream we lived in floating cities above underwater jungles
        which we did   and the Japanese protozoid
slept for a day after destroying the prehistoric insects
        we filled the Crystal Palace with wine and installed
street-accessible spigots   ghosts rose from catacombs
        to vote everything was grandfatherclocked in
circus elephants retired with lousy pensions the crime scenes
        all water-colored   roadblocks in paradise
and fake ideals on your person at all times for the authorities
        using moodrings at funerals   cockrings for nuptials
as it should be using canoes for coffins and coffins
        for ice chests   sweet incantations of the dire choir
all things in pockets of oblique   the skylines the ribcages
        of dead cattle secret maps of our cortices
polymorphs spreading their quilts in the camouflaged parks
        pixel-shimmers everywhere   no more catchers
in the blight to hold the awe-field with legend
        we fall and fall all night   we hoaxed with vibrancy
old accounts haunting the scree of our nano-lives
        we caught the last blush of a child and put it in amber
we had a museum to innocence full of blushes, apologies,
        mixed tapes, hair gels, Bazooka Joe, toy regattas
all the war horses are all now glue   rickety scaffolding
        we found the velvet underground and pissed on its
velour catching zephyrs in butterfly nets   naming them
        with Tourette's

...

morphnacular xix: syderesis of one's virtual fates

we took the Panzers apart to build the dada tetanus playgrounds
        no one has played marbles anyway for a millennium
a caravan of raincheck plans ambushed by expirations on milk cartons
        the holidays all being swept up by migrant workers
vines though still rise slowly up the columns of wire and latticework
        in the curbside weed gardens everything smelling of weed
and simple sacraments   the surgeons extracted the robots from
        within us all and we could not stop whispering our erotic
past lives to virtual wilderness creatures   we became stellar
        above ruins and stelae   the architects learning
from lab-simulated Atlantises   took all of our roadtrips
        on hits of placid and no one ever peaked   highway
by skyfare by lowbrow by dustbowl by signal flare by devil-dare
        at the thoroughfare and our passports stamped more
than welfare checks   when asked what he wanted to be
as a boy   our el presidente exclaimed that he wanted to be
a world-class skimmer   a speedreader, a water-strider
        an expert Olympic blur   we found a discount way to cross
mountain ranges by clutching the penises of weather balloons
        el presidente wore tap-shoes and sparked the tops of granite
summits   the pain dissipates as the vitriol accumulates
        we all went out to collect lightning bugs but
returned with jars of hummingbirds so all knew we were going
        straight to hell again   just like our mommas said
Orpheus couldn't adapt so got decapitated   should have stayed
        in hell   are you as shredded as the rest of us?
run as fast as you can as spools of lottery tickets coil their
        tentacles about your mathematical destiny   skim faster

. . .

morphnacular xx.: anti-ataraxia

the Buddhist one-ness balance and right way of nothingness
the vocabulary of animals is limited by proteins
as is the larvae in the flesh the parasite in the host
puppy on leash by fried chicken pit grease cracklings taunt it
the atheist watching the priest in the pulpit sweat
moray eel snapping jaws shut missing its prey retracting coil violently
Quik Trip Friday night employee under-staffed with PMS
he's driving to work "on E" no money appointment waiting
you reading this? dying alcoholic? stoned addict paraplegic?
don't be pretentious
5 tablets of ephedrine one Red Bull one coffee a chocolate bar (toffee)
splinters in feet, splinters in abdomen, splinters in neck, attacking them
huh? duh. what? slur. yadda? bleh. blech? hruumphh. ba. pffttt. blah. blah.
ready to explode to grow to kaleidoscope to emote to assault w/ color
you have lost your childhood stop making excuses you are never bored
50 cent Superball from Publix gumball machine
finals week, daily commute, unquiet mind, high blood pressure, turbines
screen door covered in fresh rain-static cat purrs dog asleep breathe deep
it's like cotton candy but I hate cotton candy it's like funnel cake maybe
I only get the voicemail on your phone. Pol Pot. Antarctica.
grass under the appendages of fire ants in their hunt light wind
what do you mean you said you appreciated my opinions? I'm what?
don't interrupt. this is rare.
something a book is comprised of? what does this word mean?
windmill wheel stuck and gears heating up creek keeps its steady flow
day after a wedding reception/going away party/punk concert/brawl
the decline of Western Civilization where's Nero and his burning violin?
the woman's womb, the amoeba's binary fission, the poet's vision
having a crush and then being crushed by the crush under a hellish bus
is this a waste of time? Jack Russell Terrier chewing on an electrical wire
lines are too long, the show will suck, the day is already fucked, grrr...
dead crow under black balloon caught on dead limb flies buzzing
my soul on its choke-chain straining to escape this husk of flesh

you in garters slowly walking towards the bed lips dominatrix red
what happens soon after devious (above) if you are lucky
got archangel's voicemail again she never home, out cavorting
televangelists, big-wave surfers, old rock-stars on tour, your mom
damsel with no tampon and run in stocking wearing white dress
drunken you dancing in the Mexican Day of the Dead parade oblivious
driving two hours for D & D dice, knowing what a Liger is, spitballs
old nags, haggard bank tellers, old pro wrestlers, colander of pintos
skydiving on a bed parachutes attached to its cast-iron frame
got the call you are coming, jump in shower, you'll be here in an hour
gave gift, cheap flowers, forgot to peel off price; she noticed
hummingbird on a string; your knee taps to guitar fret-work frenetic
adrenaline to domestic dispute handcuffs episode of COPS
parasol floats over waterfall ascends above trees through the mist
jealous that I will never be as gorgeous as her, green for her flesh
first time ever seeing snow running into the yard--sticking out tongue
tired ideas about religion, my mind after grading, long division
you in rearview mirror smiling looking at me chap-stick applying
every fiber of the horse's being simply can't get the tiny sugar-cube
parking lots surrounding the venue of next poetry reading in my dream
cocaine or the nerd sense? Confused. I wear Curad bandages and cry
when T. and I cleaned the debris thus freeing the stream at Mt. Cheaha
one time I did Perfect Duster (inhalant) and drooled and giggled....
stairwell here at the Moreland house out of Alfred Hitchcock
praline ice-cream, LEGOs, free barbecue, pocketknives, bicycle chains
after the breakup, addiction, and resignation—glad they all happened
what I am going to be if I keep writing these poor definitions
her in the morning, me + too much coffee, Rufus bereft of chew-toy
Jack Russell Terrier's eyes and posture after desecrating my flip-flops
2 packs of guitar strings, just ate hot wings, no work to do, stereo playing
so elevated internally or externally that the earth is something to laugh at
a Chinese seer read my palm in China-town in Yokohama, Japan
slow crawl up thigh intersecting fast pulse from the head in the crotch
sunflare microwave jellyfish-sting firebrand dentist's needle bourbon
pissed-off English major after the dissertation, storm angry on horizon
speed at which the Millennium Falcon flies and also Franz Liszt's fingers
William Blake's engravings on his medium of choice, printings illuminati
ignoring the indescribable no matter how annoying it gets
no matter what they do, plastic forks can't defeat the lawnmower blades
only happened to me once, and I fell for her—after that, just indifferent

do you believe the crock of shit written in the line above this
chigger in lover's skin covered & smothered with remover of nail polish
the nail of the polish, the remover of the polish, the toe of the finger
I'd rip open my chest with the crudest instrument to feel this one last time
summer. Moreland, GA. Cows in one field. Hay bails in squares adjacent
bong water, mold floating on top of it shifts from movement on couch
soul hovers outside of wardrobe waiting as you pick your outfit; see it?
no such thing. Guitar, puppy, books, beer, record player, ghosts, regrets
last night I felt it—her nose on my collarbone—she whimpers in dreams
a cross between a dog and a fucking watermelon; don't invite to party
"I don't care where the shit we eat just decide! Damn you are in a mood."
See this look I am looking at you with. How else would you describe it?
no amount of leather, money, hallucinogens is going to get me to do that
kudzu kaleidoscope gnawing light at optic nerves' root in the stomach
call me Jitters. I play cards. I know militia. My teeth chatter.
that sepia-toned frame with rust and windburn among the personal effects
teach 7 years grading essays emerge from that and say numb again assholes
the sandwich was just okay—the Genoa salami needs horseradish
no way in hell that tornado of tigers made of shattered glass will hit here
a blue speckled egg 1,000 ft. high in a nest in a redwood national forest
on edge of seat jagged radio waves blazing eyes tendons of steak knives
glass tiger tornado is going to rip the soft flesh off of all of us akimbo
vespers blast in winters pissed wild druthers turn into random whispers
time down off its crucifix of 12 there on the couch it says amazing things
I cut through fishing lines that caught the creature just to taste of its lips
the machines work better when the humans are dead
quiz shows end with tax and hit men in Vegas only the best gaffer knows
the guitar under a world of guitars saying "I am the only guitar!"
washing off wounds never was a practice we could do with music
wait six months for form to come better luck placing your work elsewhere
I look around me my elbows in cushions I realize I am in a coffin finally
burnt-out on learning-about what's new in poetry; thus, I write it again
the easy reference is wind or wolves—call this a housewife English teacher
Geddy Lee pounding me on the bridge of my nose with pulsing bass lines
Keats, 21, doing laundry one day, coughing blood on white handkerchief
she rarely is, if ever, though we've fed her delicacies held in gold leaf paper
never saw it until my firstborn coming out of the womb (I've never seen)
it worked out—we moved in together—we were in a less bleak forever
dog distempered third world country shantytown dirt road flies buzzing
that time I was so into you took wrong exit near Newnan drove 20 miles

summer descends through pollen landing on trees' afros as we lie beneath
neck tied to the invisible noose slung from my computer keyboard all day
bridge cables during an earthquake as the concrete snake contorts beneath
that babbling sonuvabitch is still in office and we still killing young men
I feel your pain but may not help you carry that lodestone dwarfstar anvil
got a job, a roof, a woman, a guitar, a (meager) talent, a steady heartbeat
remember high school varsity football practice after long scrimmage
man at MARTA bus stop contemplating—spied on him at red light
truckers, single moms, racing dogs, engines of muscle of the great machine
they say I am in the head; I say, "touch this;" next: police or ambulance
why do you insist on jumping on the trampoline on the crumbling cliff?
nothing is at this point in my life and sometimes I find that to be…
always write no matter the block punch the complacent clock with lyric
the orbs either cascade or merge or collide—do they do all of this at once or is it
                                                                          a lie?

. . .

morphnacular xxi.: galaxy structures, parts of a feather, parts of an insect's mouth, a museum burning, and general parts of a sage thrasher

structure of contour feather   are not radically distributed in space
          supercluster   1 million distributions   years aren't light they lie
retrices   coverts   remiges   upper and lowerlore
          eyebrow thrasher of the sage stripe   super-cluster of night nape
hemipteran in the small Magellanic Clouds   no structures larger than super-clusters
          lies, all lies   barbs, rachis, aftershaft, vane   hooklet vs. barbule
labrum vs. labium   about 90 percent of space seems to consist of bubble-like voids
          the Boötes void   superclusters occur at the intersections of sheets and filaments
maxilla and mandible   stars have compound eyes
maxillary palp
          probiscus guards nectar and adds nectar to nectar to super-cluster
megaparsecs of nectarines   overwhelmed ocellus   for sucking blood
          you need equipment   for eating stars
hypopharynx
voids sheets filaments   lowerlore   upperlore   innerlore
lorical

•

vector vexed vector vexed vexed vexed vector vexed hexagon vector vex-vapor mech-vex
          hex mixed hex mixed mixed schism hex vex vector hex megaton mech vector
vexed vector vexed hex hexed proctor never text never text never text erect mechs
          selectravix mega-mix vector vector never vex proctor proctor mechanize

prosper
never text always mechanize to prosper prospectahex vexataprompt always proctor
hex vex hex vex propulgate vector mystic hectors heckle hexagons nega-
mech
vexation hextacle rector props rector props vex-mechs prompt rectors' texts hex-
mech
all vex ex-ed all integers heved vexation upon prospect mixed mech and
text

•

sculptor, photographer, performance artist draw and paint with a facility of
tribute styles
cities scrawl-paved   a city of elipses   a soundbyte up your
figurative ass
nique hurts, always has   superficial shimmer for illustrated
urbana
bridges and spans   Monet-lengths   clouds teach one to
put a brush down
a garden is mostly chance   a painting is mostly chance   a
decision is okra
ovoid begun in the blitz   during the pre pyre-war years
themes gleam
terracotta maquettes   "Monet is an eye, but only an eye"
reconstruct the mud
the perception of light changes the subject through time
so know owls
there's no view from above   there never has been a view from above
merge your sub
a picture is a something that looks out on a window   laugh before
thee choke
never study art in Brussels   never burn tubas   irrelevant Soviet spies
interlude
an image at odds with its title is the easiest way to histrionics but power
corrupts
the arch is large   arc swords/triumphal scimitars   do work that can be
walked through
and splayed around   hinge bones and know portents
shaman paint
in the best jobs they pay you millions to contribute to the death of your own

culture bitches

     precocious post-impressionist   totemic sexuality"nothing to
fix one's gaze upon, everything escapes"   "there is no such thing as a
good painting about nothing"

     flat forms reveal truth   "silence is so accurate"   cursory
glance
laden with latent doom   verticals reared   messianic subjugation
subjective core-
     relative   fraud, genius, madman, surrealist, moustache   eerie
coastlines in rigid
retina kinesis   make all art by manipulating steam   art that hangs
everywhere   sky-canvas
     op art options   mix the pigment with molten wax   layer
the flags
oldenburgian floorburgers   taste like   conformed citizenry
drive on thru
     "decapitated rabbits, exploding umbrellas, raped beds"
unfound art is best
we can modulate color to create the experience of viewing the flats as 3-d's
     polish palpable or superficial   spoonerisms   dada
pork chops
carnies tear down the museums and replace with rusted county fair rides
cotton candy
     low cost and mass produced   one must eradicate the illusion of
depth beyond brushstrokes   idyll-yearning   calculate angles of
30, 45, and 60 degrees
     he never sold a painting in his lifetime   you can paint your
way into the subatomic world but not your way out of   the gouache
fermenting on the fromage
     under-pinned in the welter   "a forest tangled with an
undergrowth of -isms"
you like to keep your imagination on a leash   it wines theories all not makes
nada
     existential was no cul-de-sac   it was a drained pool   with a dark
crack
i was called a paradisiac   not sure if it was a compliment   i
walked into gold
     demi-monde is postmodern sherbert flavor   "the red vine is very
beautiful. I have hung it in one of our rooms"   he painted Henriette
confectionary for the ears

violence is an aircraft you love to fly on faster than seasons' violences
a priveleged found object must be as transformed as a non-priv in order for us to
feel trans
sending your best cartoons by pneumatic tube salutes   salads by
lunch apnia
turpentine on Magna leaves best paintings i'd swear to gods trace lights
of infrared skin tones   reference   distillation
album spins
the viewer   be selective in your use of dots   reality has sticky
translucent succulent
                                        lips   eyes
mostly lips   (jaws)

                                ●

engraver, violinist, cartographer   draughtsman-illustrator and
printmaker
        had the ability to levitate expert in animal-husbandry   my
apparatchik satchel
my luminous tool-cravat burner of museums   resurrector of museums
        ninja minimalist of scalpel brushstrokes   sketch the
secret tunnels
idiosyncratic indie-savior savant   solar system tats   claptrap supremacism
        anonymous traffic with specific radio scribbles   killed a priest with a
palette knife
insignia vista carved into forearm short-circuit and writhe in a river bed
        i had a pocket full of hypercubes i was convulsing with beauty
psycho-guide
pleasure has more gravity in you than in others   and we all carry you
know this
        i shot across the city with my scythe cutting all the elevator cables falling
starlets
decalcomania   but i stuck, got stuck   between two sheets   was
made not unto art
    covered in alpaca   electrocuted   scraped from the crime-scene
wiped on cave-wall
"thinking about death led me to create monsters that both attracted and repelled
me"
        you built an imaginary helicopter and sent it into battle with an invisble
one

i could smell the ascertation   when they ask you what it is, just call it
"merz"
      the only difference between painting a living person or a dead one is the
gaze
bilboquet scared my gorilla   made me have an inner gorilla   i paint during
chess, ashamed
      the breeze has no tongues I can't translate some wear garlands i wear
empires
duchampions of cubist and futurist fusions   my primordialism on the
rectilinear grid
      fragments most   no one lives ere long beyond the
densities
single yellow planes   line the field of vision   like unfurled
realities
      a photographer, Dadaist, maker of relish for brats   the
Rayographer
an iron with spikes on its face teaches us to look at wrinkles with reverance or
that seeing is sharp
      i launch my blue lines and give you   oh never call this
skyscraper a flower
i wove all of the afars into   never you betchas   sold tickets   to
the patio of dullards
      the flower was never your vagina you can't stick your dick in the flower
dullard
slaves try to struggle from the half-worked marble blocks   as best they can
without
      it is touching bt not life-affirming   get up and fuck your fancy car
with a dick made of X's   X's and their chromosones   why's and
their eggs
      a Cubist never repents   thanks God   fo' strategy of
greys
gloom gloam   foal lapse   loom hive   horde gloam   revolt swarm
swoon-womb

•

arpeggio with scintillating superstring conflagaration
      hovering amidst the life about me like a seahorse drifting
      i only wanted to make new musical instruments but had
to flip patties

as my own sundial i wonder who stands to read my day or days--
who reads the cavernous malaise? bored with virtual games in
my tongs.
i left the zoo to become an architect and built new
books with vomit
of metals in them, good books of ore with great alloys employable by the super-
structures
i once had to have a plesiosaur removed from my heart.
they took the bones and laid them out like my stitches.
i bellowed with sawdust, glitter, and powder
from my lips
i wished i could have been as honorable as a dinosaur.

•

"Even the gods cowered like dogs at what they had done."

The Epic of Gilgamesh, translated by Herbert Mason

•

"Strange things have been spoken; why does
Your heart speak strangely? The dream was

Marvelous but the terror was great; we must
Treasure the dream whatever the terror."

The Epic of Gilgamesh, translated by N.K. Sanders

•

"He looked at the walls,
Awed at the heights
His people had achieved
And for a moment—just a moment—
All that lay behind him
Passed from view."

The Epic of Gilgamesh, translated by Herbert Mason

•

"Hold my hand in yours, and we will not fear what hands like ours can do."

The Epic of Gilgamesh, translated by Danny P. Jackson

What We Wrote On The City's Walls

I will never kill a beautiful mythic beast for you. Sorry.

I made you an incredible stapler of dimensions.

It's a sorta terrible teeming succulent sortie life.

Death is a 64-ounce tub of plastic full of butter.

We were real skywriters—our biplanes spraying blue ether.

Under the thick bark of the trees were panels of circuit boards.

While falling to the earth, the safe flew by; I still thought of cracking it.

Our eyes are not bloodshot—don't you know evolution when you see it?

The water in the lagoon was smooth surrendering hands. Evade.

I will transfer you to the ass-end of the cornfield if you speak of it.

There's no recording the horrors of the passing bus windows.

Arroyos of despots, hats to wear while crossing them. Goggles.

Weaving your nets, always braiding, you existential mock-up.

The only thing you learned from a life of ornithoptery was narcolepsy.

The sin-eaters arrive in Vegas, the only place they are allowed to sin.

Our skin became yarn—a Penelope-stash—we make tapestries.

Slake and swagger artisan——your great weapon——holography.

Do not remove said mouthpiece. If you do, the force-feeding ceaseless.

A pomegranate has 613 seeds, grown in the wild. We have short winters.

It was easy. We just made vampires drain themselves. Done.

Trying was no good. So I spelunked. Chasm-wise, I said, "Prep."

Expunging into my dermis this tube of toxins I made from Latin.

Your vehicle is my vehicle. Thus, I must destroy us both. Mat of welcome.

Of the zoos of the universe, you would be housed among dandruff.

My face burned off and I asked for the mask to walk away slower.

I cut your hair in the dark and you commented on the floor of ears.

I tried to kill the obelisk. It was patient. It handed me a dartboard.

That taste in your mouth is the same taste in the mouth of a Sumerian slave.

I know nothing about Sumeria or slavery—I just want a taste.

I made you a thing that can't be named and will you attach it to lineage?

I am sure about this: most of us are centipedes with few legs.

I am trying to turn my body into a propeller. It hurts. It's hard.

I kill deer by running beside them. They see me, have heart-attacks.

I want to make mandalas mandatory. That's how crazy I swan.

A butterfly's tastebuds are located on its legs. Poets take walks.

I take a dose. I consider if everyone has taken it. I politic then.

All my battleships are in my chest-of-drawers. Bad-ass tats.

My hope-chest is a campfire. It burns albums and regalia.

Rifle in hand. Rifle fires. Rifle kills cloud. Things land. Cotton. Ruffle.

The things that got shot in clouds fall down upon us. Synchronize.

I sat on a couch poor long enough until they hoisted me.

All of my books are great ships of my reading. They find shores in snowglobes.

The swarm flew to warn. Then it flew to swarm. Then it nested in us.

Swim as far out as you can. Look back. That's your cramp.

Lyric has a place where it sits there with no tongue or ears.

We help lyric out like mechanics as best we can with our drugs.

I am holding an oval. I am scared. It seems to ovulate with no vulvacore.

Kachina. Patina of scrubland where all windshields crack.

I doll. I dollop burnt doll unto glass eyes. I dearst. I doll-up. I blingle.

Cedar is good. Pine as well. Avoid contractors. Cut your own. Ire and awl.

I made syrup from a burnt-down house. I smoked moonshine with it.

I once thought I needed armor. Now I know I just need passwords.

I fell from the heavens on the waves of whalesong landing on a desk.

I skateboard into the abyss and still get injured. I give it substances.

I lost trust in the nest and gave eggs to miserly proofs—waiting for pot leaves.

I recently saw the white shroud of all walk up to me. It asked. I said it.

I saw a celebrity out at sea—I tried to drown it in its own treasury.

It takes patience, waiting for a universe to cool so you can stab someone with it.

The devil in a birdcage or wearing a bikini was the old model. Now cellphone apps.

This incredible book of poems fell from the aurora borealis, but I lost it.

The iceberg had the artifact in it. We waited for it to melt—we couldn't wait.

We started chipping away the ice for our sweet-teas and swollen joints.

We left town before we ever got to the core. Wonder where to get more good ice?

Like ice-fishing—cut a hole—drop the hook down into the dark abyss.

The culture advanced after we eighty-sixed all the exorcists.

The foolproof city was forever unpopulated. We admire from the afar.

The pistachio, a most perfect invention. That's genius, not this engine.

My spine was an electric fence that a herd of substances leaned against.

The brains of most of us were toy pianos waiting for those alien children.

I took a filigree from a filibuster and stabbed it into a Day-Glo soundbyte.

Piebald hellhole bullet-holed with random media I love your scattershot blanket.

There's not a spade in the whole wilderness left with an edge on it. No men.

I feel like an awl drenched in honey and dredged in history to amber.

Oh how I love a maze at end of winter. Snow thawing. The melt southernly.

What's wild is that the wrecking ball is us watching TV. Impact. Crumble.

Accelerate downhill with amnesia into the well with its gleaming teeth.

Or start the car listless towards the coffee shop where that girl or guy works.

The bees fucking quit. Damn. Why? No one knows, but the bees fucking quit.

A man wrote the tyranny of email, and I wrote the synecdoche of spam.

A computer can't misspell. It's fucked-up. The thing can't not misspell.

The cancer has a lion's mane or hyena laugh. Cancer always has offices.

Crickets midgets kismet widgets spankings chemo samples—all at the grocery.

I never started smoking until the apocalypse. I eat ashes like cud.

I love this free-flying jetpack that elevates me so high I can edit this poem.

I know how to make a sock-puppet be a world-leader or moppet.

I love the fuck out of a good bass-line—makes me look towards horizons.

A planet in a catcher's mitt. A moon-landing in a sandwich. A cosmos in a sauce.

To be a tendon in a deer's loin as it's hunted with bow drawn to tension.

I have worn my coveralls. I have been hunted. Killed. Reborn. Your camou don't work.

Make your escape with whispers and starships. Make your secrets earthen.

You will be back. You never left. Break bones to make science. Breathe in.

The crack in the dam is a fate you watch over and over in horror films.

This is the best father with wings you have ever had or ever will.

The ash of snow or the snow of white petals downs the hopeful cracked earth.

Driving past the airstrip on the two-lane highway a swirl of turkey vultures

Disturbed by a single-engine plane lifting vicariously with its student pilot.

It's just linguistic filigree. You'd text-message Jesus and treat him as a bookie.

Savvy tech-altar. Ingenious sympodium. Fiber optic baptism. Thanks you congod.

Eight per cent of women are left-handed, and the rest are just lying about guns.

An insane amount of insurmountable beauty just overtook me. I press cape overwhelm.

I make a waffle of beauty and look at it. Don't take a pic. Don't eat. Appreciate. Serape.
I killed a man once. I killed every man once. I lived beyond. A man killed that next.

A man wrote on the walls after killing the bulls of heaven that he lost the secret

To immortality due to narcolepsy, but ironically, he was wrong—stalwart strode into mythos.

. . .

A Note on the Form of the Prose-Poems of Tattered Scrolls And Postulates

Tattered Scrolls and Postulates, Vol. 1, began around six years ago, out in a small house in Moreland, Georgia. I started to come home at night, after teaching several literature and composition courses, and just write, freeform and stream of consciousness, into one word document, just ripping from margin to margin. I would tell people who asked that I was working on something, that I was writing, but I always felt like a liar because it was mainly just an outlet for my kinetic energy and apparent mania. About a year later, as I was cleaning out my desktop, I came across this file—about 40 pages of one relentless straight rant from one side of the page to the other—a giant block of text.

I started to read it, and then I started to experiment with breaking some of it into stanzas. I decided to try eight line stanzas first, and I even tried to convert it to hexameter. Then, I noticed a pattern—somewhere along the way, in this mess of a text, I had begun to end each line when the margin forced me to—at the end of the allowed number of characters for the basic one-inch margin, as it were— there was a weird syntax developing there—a fragmented dialect that had its own jagged music to me. In other words, each line had to stand on its own as a poem or story impended upon by that margin.

I decided to try ten line stanzas just to see what would happen. I started chopping the chunk up, moving lines around, whole sections around, etc. Then, I decided that the basic Times New Roman font in a standard Word document WOULD BE my form—not very innovative, I know, but what happened was that, as I would end the line, and the line would bleed over into the next, I would begin to "backwards edit" the line so that it would fit the format of the basic nine by eleven page. This created strange new phrasings for me within the lines themselves because of the omission choices I had to go back and make. It was then that I started to think of each line as a possible one-line short story which worked by itself and within the stanza as a whole, and then I started to think of the stanzas ALSO all working together as a whole narrative—a book-length poem.

This was the impetus of Tattered Scrolls and Postulates. Trying to write 100 10-lined stanzas, made up of lines which are, supposedly, each-unto-themselves, one-line short stories, is a bit insane, I know—this idea may have failed, as a feat of expertise or technique, but I think what resulted from trying this is a book that I can be very proud of. Overall, the book is about someone who has accidentally downloaded or been purposefully implemented with a great knowledge of the universe and human experience; however, this wealth of knowledge does not seem to help our speaker navigate his life better—in many ways, it makes it worse. This text, in my forties, allowed me to burn the pyre of all of my influences, interests, confluences, obsessions, pleasures, and anxieties—it was a truly cathartic undertaking whose energy I hope is infectious and useful for the reader.

Acknowledgements

These poems may have been edited to suit the final version of this collection, so they may appear differently than their original appearances in journals.

"Primordial Vesicle" was previously published in Contemporary American Voices

Sections 1-4 of "Tattered Scrolls and Postulates" were previously published in an interview with 32 Poems

Sections 5-9 of "Tattered Scrolls and Postulates" were previously published in Contemporary American Voices

Section 10 of "Tattered Scrolls and Postulates" was previously published at Plumberries Press

Section 11 of "Tattered Scrolls and Postulates" was previously published at Golden Isles Weekly Read

Section 12 "Tattered Scrolls and Postulates" was previously published at experiential-experimental-literature

Section 13 of "Tattered Scrolls and Postulates" was previously published at Black Heart Magazine

Section 14 of "Tattered Scrolls and Postulates" was previously published at experiential-experimental-literature

Section 15 of "Tattered Scrolls and Postulates" was previously published at Belle Reve Literary Journal

Sections 16-21 of "Tattered Scrolls and Postulates" were previously published at of/with

Sections 22 and 23 of "Tattered Scrolls and Postulates" were previously published at Belle Reve Literary Journal

Sections 24-26 of "Tattered Scrolls and Postulates" were previously published at The Song Is

Section Section 27 of "Tattered Scrolls and Postulates" was previously published at Zaira Journal

Section 28 of "Tattered Scrolls and Postulates" was previously published at TUCK magazine

Section 29 of "Tattered Scrolls and Postulates" was previously published at Your One Phone Call

Section Section 30 of "Tattered Scrolls and Postulates" was previously published at Zaira Journal

Sections 31-33 of "Tattered Scrolls and Postulates" were previously published at Otoliths

Section 34 of "Tattered Scrolls and Postulates" was previously published at TUCK magazine

Section Section 35 of "Tattered Scrolls and Postulates" was previously published at Crack the Spine

Sections 37 and 38 of "Tattered Scrolls and Postulates" were previously published at Absinthe Poetry Review

Section 40 of "Tattered Scrolls and Postulates" was previously published at Unbroken

Sections 45-48 of "Tattered Scrolls and Postulates" were previously published at Birds Piled Loosely

Sections 49 and 50 of "Tattered Scrolls and Postulates" were previously published at Zaira Journal

Section 53 of "Tattered Scrolls and Postulates" was previously published at Dark

Matter

Section 54 of "Tattered Scrolls and Postulates" was previously published at 13 Myna Birds

Sections 56 and 57 of "Tattered Scrolls and Postulates" were previously published at Baldhip

Section 59 of "Tattered Scrolls and Postulates" was previously published at Futures Trading

Sections 61 and 62 of "Tattered Scrolls and Postulates" were previously published at Card Alpha

Sections 63 and 64 of "Tattered Scrolls and Postulates" were previously published at UFO Gigolo

Sections 65-69 of "Tattered Scrolls and Postulates" were previously published at Otoliths

Sections 70-75 of "Tattered Scrolls and Postulates"were previously published at Heron Clan

Section 76 of "Tattered Scrolls and Postulates" was previously published at penwheel

Sections 77-80 of "Tattered Scrollsand Postulates" were previously published at Blue Mountain Review

Section 81 of "Tattered Scrolls and Postulates" was previously published at UFO Gigolo

Sections 83-85 of "Tattered Scrolls and Postulates" were previously published at Futures Trading

Sections 86-88 of "Tattered Scrolls and Postulates" were previously published at Blue Mountain Review

Sections 89-91 of "Tattered Scrolls and Postulates" were previously published at Ink In Thirds

Sections 96-100 of "Tattered Scrolls and Postulates" were previously published at HELIOS

"morphnacular i.: anagnorisis" and "morphnacular ii. : Bono postcard hamartia" were previously published at Sein and Weirden

"morphnacular iii.: bus-ride peripeteia" was published in Wild Goose Poetry Review

"morphnacular vi.: annunaki dysphemism", "morphnacular vii.: midlife hypophora", and "morphnacular viii.: homo sapiens sapiens meiosis" were previously published in the Cricket Online Review

"morphnacular x.: golden age paraprosdokian" was previously published by Forklift, Ohio

"morphnacular xi.: Empedocles and the apis" was previously published by Otoliths

"morphnacular xii.: Lacanian mutatis mutantis" was previously published in Squawkback

"morphnacular xiii.: Axis of Andriambahomanana", "morphnacular xiv.: Albuquerque waffle house hodoiporeo", and "morphnacular xv.: choroplethic hypsometric isopleth" were previously published at Otoliths

"morphnacular xviii: perlecutionary act of denizens", "morphnacular xix: universal instantiation of mass charlantanism", and "morphnacular xx: syderesis of one's virtual fates" were previously published at Vector Press

"What We Wrote On The City's Walls" was previously published in Gulper Eel

Lightning Source UK Ltd.
Milton Keynes UK
UKOW04f0109140917

309165UK00002B/87/P